Gotta Shop!

50 or so great little places in the D.C. Metro area

PAULA COUPE

Attic Window Publishing, Inc.
Alexandria, VA

Attic Window Publishing, Inc. Alexandria, VA 22304

© 2004 by Paula Mayes Coupe
All rights reserved.

Front cover design © 2004 Peggy Archambault
Interior design and illustrations by Vincent Hughes
All rights reserved.

Printed in the United States of America
10 9 8 7 6 5 4 3 2 1

Library of Congress Control Number: 2004115739

ISBN: 0-9722274-0-7

Publisher's Note:
Neither Attic Window Publishing, Inc., nor the author has any interest, financial or personal, in the locations listed in this book. No fees were paid or services rendered in exchange for inclusion in these pages. As time passes, store ownership may change and hours may vary. It is advisable to call ahead before making a visit.

*For my grandmother, Helen Payne Gibbons,
who let me carry her shopping bags.*

Preface

Please use this little book to get away from the malls and into the neighborhoods… away from the big box stores and mass retailing and into intimate and individual shopping experiences…away from "hum drum" and on to "hey wow."

Before I ever thought about writing this book, I would prowl around the malls and look at the same old things in the same old stores. As a matter of fact, wherever you go in America you can probably find a mall or a Wal-Mart and they all look alike. There's a comfort in sameness—that's why lots of Americans go to Paris and eat at McDonalds (not me!).

But this book shook me up! My shopping companions and I started visiting strange neighborhoods, we read maps, we got lost, we stumbled into experiences that we never would have had at Tysons Corner. Not only did I find new communities in my home town, I was lucky to meet lots of admirable owners, many of whom had quit comfortable jobs, cashed in their 401(k)s, and mortgaged their houses to follow their entrepreneurial dreams. These are brave people, who deserve our admiration and consideration.

Please use this book to meet them yourself. If you're looking for a gift, frequent the small, out-of-the way places. Take the time to browse and buy, if it strikes your fancy and you can afford it. You'll be helping to keep communities vibrant and supporting enterprises that are in a position to really deliver that special service we find so elusive today.

Please venture away from your neighborhood. We are so lucky to live in a metropolis comprising three jurisdictions with invisible borders. Feel free to move around, discover unknown areas. You can't get too lost—you'll eventually run into the beltway!

And Thank You...

What's a shopping trip without a friend? I began shopping at a very early age with my grandmother, Helen. We would go downtown and wander up and down F Street, visiting Jelleff's, Kann's, Lansburgh's, Woodward and Lothrop, Hecht's, and Garfinkel's. She would buy something—a hat, a dress, a coat, a pair of shoes—and we'd have lunch at Reeve's or the Lansburgh Tea Room and go home. She'd look at the item for a week and then we'd go back downtown and take it back. The next week, we'd start again! We used to call it "prowling around," and we did it for 40 years.

But, since she's gone to the big mall in heaven, I have lots of friends with whom I now prowl, and/or who have recommended places to prowl for this book. Here's a list (in alphabetical order): Louise Abbruzzese, Beth Alvarez,

Karen Beach, Patti Becker, Nancy Beiging, Rachel Branger, LaVerne Collins, Brian Coupe (my long-suffering husband who hates to shop), Ann Farson, Ann Figura, Trish Gibson, Nancy Hall, Knowles Harper, O.J. Hazard, Penny Heiston, Barbara Humes, Fred Isbister, Paulette (PK) Johnson, Robyn Krauthammer, Rolfe Larson, Erin Madden, Jean Maddox, Jennifer Marks, Melissa McAdams (who traveled from Knoxville, TN), Peggy Orser, Joanna Rubini, Joan Schindel, Elizabeth Shaw, Beverlee Stafford, Kelly St. Clair, Kerry Sutton, Karen Wheeless, Martha Wilcox, and Cherie Wilderrotter.

I know I probably forgot someone, but a thousand thanks to everyone for your help and listening to me say, "I'm almost finished with the book," a thousand times.

And a very special thank you to my Attic Window publishers, Bill Tabor and Elise Fulstone, for their thoughtful editing and always believing that I really would finish this book.

Please be aware that exchange and return policies at small, independently owned stores may be different from big chain stores. Check before you buy.

Please know that every attempt has been made to ensure the information about each and every shop and eatery is as current and correct as possible—but things do change. So, if something isn't the way it should be, please forgive us.

Contents

- vi   **Preface**
- **1   DISTRICT OF COLUMBIA**
- **2   Capitol Hill**
  - 2   Eastern Market
  - 5   Art and Soul
  - 5   A. Litteri, Inc.
- **6   Eighth Street, SE**
  - 7   Backstage, Inc.
  - 8   Alvear Studio
  - 9   Plaid
- **10   14th & U Streets**
  - 10   go mama go
  - 11   Home Rule
  - 13   The Garden District
  - 14   Pulp
  - 15   Nana
  - 16   Millennium Decorative Arts
  - 16   Zawadi
  - 17   Meeps
  - 17   Wild Women Wear Red
- **19   Georgetown**
  - 20   Pirjo
  - 21   Dream Dresser
  - 22   A Mano
  - 23   Rooms with a View
- **24   Dupont Circle**
  - 24   The Written Word
  - 26   Second Story Books

28 Toast and Strawberries

30 Adams Morgan
30 Daisy
31 A Little Shop of Flowers
32 All About Jane

33 Foxhall Square
33 Tree Top Toys
35 Abrielle
36 Pamela Barkley

37 Cleveland Park
38 Wake Up Little Susie
39 Artisan Lamp Company

39 Friendship Heights
40 The Point of It All
42 Finials
43 Periwinkle, Inc.
44 Catch Can

45 Museum Shops
45 The Arthur M. Sackler Gallery of Art
46 The National Building Museum
47 The Museum of Women in the Arts

49 MARYLAND

50 Bethesda
50 Montgomery Farm Woman's Cooperative Market
51 Three Dog Bakery

53 Bethesda—Chevy Chase
53 Sylene

55 Bethesda—Wildwood Shopping Center
55 Red Orchard

56 ZYZXY

Wheaton
58 Barry's Magic Shop, Ltd.
60 Bonifant Books
60 The Jewish Bookstore of Greater Washington
61 Barbarian
62 The Little Bitts Shop
63 Showcase Aquarium
65 The Toy Exchange
66 Shalom Strictly Kosher Market

Takoma Park
67 House of Musical Traditions
67 Finewares
67 Polly Sue's Vintage Shop

Hyattsville
70 Franklin's

Mt. Rainier
71 GLUT Food Co-op
74 Nisey's Boutique

Oxon Hill
76 Desserts by Gerard

Thurmont
78 Discount Fabrics

Davidsonville
80 Homestead Gardens
82 Tropic Bay Water Gardens

VIRGINIA

Alexandria—Old Town
86 The Alexandria Farmers' Market
88 The Torpedo Factory Arts Center

89	Why Not?
90	La Cuisine—The Cook's Resource
90	Gossypia
91	Elder Crafters of Alexandria, Inc.

92 Alexandria—Old Town, West of Washington (WOW)

92	Ten Thousand Villages
93	Kingsbury Chocolates
94	J Brown & Co
94	The Lamplighter
95	A Likely Story

95 Alexandria—Del Ray

96	Del Ray Farmers' Market
96	Tops of Old Town, Inc.
97	Bonnie Greer & Company
98	Eight Hands Round
98	Remix
99	Potomac West Interiors & Antique Gallery
99	Five Oaks Antiques
100	Eclectic Nature

102 Alexandria—Hollin Hall

102	Hollin Hall Variety Store, Inc.
104	The Blossom Shop

105 Arlington—Crystal City

106	Ship's Hatch, Inc.
107	The Men's Shop Ltd.
108	Crystal Boutique

109 Arlington—Lee Heights Shops

109	Pastries by Randolph
110	Arrowine
110	Kinder Haus Toys
111	Prince Street

- 111 Lemon Chiffon & Lemon Twist
- 112 Pamela Wright Interiors
- 112 Imagination Station
- 113 Lee Heights Florist
- 113 Facets

115 McLean
- 115 Mae's Dress Boutique
- 116 The Artisans

118 Falls Church
- 118 Foxes Music
- 119 Upscale Resale Quality Consignments
- 121 Fairfax Glass Company
- 121 Woodburners Two

123 Vienna
- 123 Star's Beads, Ltd.
- 124 Consignment Boutique
- 125 The Brambled Nest
- 125 The Artful Gift Shop
- 126 Earth and Fire

127 Springfield
- 127 Fischer's Hardware

128 Occoquan
- 129 Hawthorne House
- 130 Details by Ursula
- 131 Brambles

132 Purcellville
- 132 Samuel S. Case

135 Index

District of Columbia

Capitol Hill

One of the oldest residential communities in the city, Capitol Hill began as Jenkins Hill—a high point in the middle of a swamp. Pierre L'Enfant picked this site for our fledgling nation's capital in 1790. In the beginning, no one wanted to live here, so boarding houses provided temporary housing for the men running our country. Eventually, these were replaced by tree-lined streets of row houses in varied architectural styles—most have been charmingly renovated. With its commercial strip bordering Pennsylvania Avenue, Capitol Hill is a lively neighborhood with a palpable sense of history.

Eastern Market
7th Street and North Carolina Avenue, SE
Washington, DC 20003
www.easternmarket.net

South Hall
(produce, flowers, baked goods, delicatessens, and Market Lunch)
Tues-Fri: 10-6, Sat: 8-6, Sun: 8-4

Market 5 Gallery
(visual and performing arts)
Tues-Fri: 11-5, Sat-Sun: 10-5

Weekend Market Festival
(arts, crafts, antiques, flea market)
Sat-Sun: 10-5

Eastern Market has been a Washington institution since it was built in 1873. Today, after fighting closure several times, it is the city's only surviving 19th century public market that is still in continuous operation. And, just as it was then, it is still one of the big attractions in the Capitol Hill area.

Adolph Cluss designed the Italianate South Hall with numerous doors and windows, a high ceiling, and no heat to accommodate an open plan for stalls. One market in a city-wide market system, Eastern Market was built as a post-Civil War civic improvement, meant to draw residents to the area. When the market expanded in 1907 with additions of the North and Center Halls (both designed by Snowden Ashford), Eastern Market truly became the town center of Capitol Hill.

Eastern Market has survived the downturn in Capitol Hill development in the 1920's, the arrival of the grocery chains, and the city's decision to close all markets in the 1950's. Now, it is owned and managed by a private organization, with several non-profits working to protect and restore this vital city landmark.

You can visit Eastern Market today, and relive its past glory. The South Hall still functions as it was designed: an open area with stalls that sell meat, eggs, produce, and other foodstuffs. Every Saturday and Sunday, farmers from around the region bring their goods to the market to satisfy the appetites of residents and

District of Columbia

tourists. (Believe it or not, members of my family with farms in Southern Maryland are still coming to market every Saturday.) The North Hall, which was once a fish market and tearoom, is now the Market 5 Gallery, an arts and community center.

Although open during the workweek (it's a popular lunch spot for nearby workers), the market expands considerably on weekends with outdoor stalls around the original building and a flea market across the street in the lots around Hine Junior High. Along with traditional market items, you can find just about anything you want at Eastern Market. You may notice that several of the shop owners in this book started out with stalls in Eastern Market. Jewelry, glassware, tableware, paintings, interesting antiques, garden ornaments, handmade soaps, and clothing only scratch the surface of the goods for sale. The flea market alone has room for 175 vendors.

What's to eat?

If you get tired in mid-shop, stop by the **Market Lunch** for a delicious crabcake sandwich. It might be hard to get a seat, but it's worth the wait. There are also several restaurants nearby that have outdoor dining if it's one of those perfect Washington days.

Art and Soul
225 Pennsylvania Avenue, SE
Washington, DC 20003
202-548-0105
Mon-Sat: 11-6 (until 7 on Thurs)

Whenever my grandmother needed a pick-me-up, she would go out and buy a hat: I buy earrings.

Art and Soul is an homage to contemporary wearable art, jewelry, and crafts. Not only are there enough earrings to cure any blue funk, there are wonderful clothes, interesting gifts, and a few well-designed occasional tables and attractive lamps, and a chair or two.

A. Litteri, Inc.
517-519 Morse Street, NE
Washington, DC 20002
202-544-0183, 202-544-0184
www.litteris.com
Tues-Weds: 8-4, Thurs-Fri: 8-5, Sat: 8-3

What's behind those green doors? Just a little piece of Italy named Litteri's. Since 1926, this exceptional market has provided Washingtonians with Italian products and excellent service.

If you are looking for pasta, there's a wall covered with about 20 types—from angel hair to ziti. The wine section has closeouts and overstocks for $2.99 a bottle along with a wide selection of Italian and domestics at 10% off the case price. If you can't choose, Mike, the store manager, who knows the stock like the back of his hand after 20 years, can put together a mixed case for you to try. Need a little olive oil? There's an entire section, right next to the balsamic vinegar shelves. Then stroll on down the shelves of sauces and spices, olives and canned tomatoes—everything is here for a great Italian meal.

In the back is the deli with homemade sausage, bacala (salted cod fish), cold cuts, fresh mozzarella (di buffola is best), parmesan, pecorino, and provolone. If you are having a party, you can order a tasty party platter or a six-foot Italian cold-cut sub, or if you are just hungry, take away a regular for your lunch.

*Also on Capitol Hill, see **Pulp on the Hill** (listed in 14th and U Streets).*

8th Street, SE

*Also known as Barracks Row, because of its proximity to the Navy Yard and the Marine Barracks, 8th Street was a vibrant neighborhood at the turn of the 20th century. Later, it turned bad, like many other neighborhoods in the city, but, proof that what goes around comes around, it's resurging once again. With brick sidewalks, plantings, and new shops and restaurants popping up all the time, it's just a short stroll from Eastern Market and a great place to visit once again, particularly on **Second Saturday**, a* *monthly event where many of the shops host parties, introduce new artists, and stay open until 9 p.m.*

Backstage, Inc.
*545 8th Street, SE
Washington, DC 20003
202-544-5744
www.backstagebooks.com
Mon-Sat: 11-7, (Halloween, 11-8)*

Have you ever wanted to be a fence? No, I don't mean someone who traffics stolen goods, but a real fence? Sandy can make you look like one. Or an Elizabethan princess, or Dracula, or just about anyone or anything else you want. No, she's not a magician or a witch, Sandy Duraes is the costume maker at Backstage, Inc., as well as its co-owner with her husband, Sandro.

Backstage has been around since 1981, but moved from Dupont Circle in 1999. (I can't imagine what that move was like!) It lives up to its reputation as "The Performing Arts Store" because it has everything needed to be a star—and plenty of local artists shop here!

After you get through the incredible collection of theater books and scripts, you can choose your part and

"Have you ever wanted to be a fence?"

get what you need to get into character. There are dialect tapes for that perfect foreign accent,

Ben Nye professional makeup, hair, wigs (all colors), mustaches, beards, masks (custom-made are available), dancewear, shoes, and real turkey feather boas in a wide range of colors. You can buy or rent costumes for both kids and adults, so everyday can be Halloween at your house.

This little shop on the corner is a place to go to be someone or something else. The only problem you may have is deciding who or what you want to be.

Alvear Studio
705 8th Street, SE
Washington, DC 20003
202-546-8434
www.alvearstudio.com
Tues-Thurs: 11-7, Fri: 11-8, Sat: 11-7,
  Sun: 12-5

Chris Alvear loves his location so much he's expanding. Then, he can add more wonderful items to his already eclectic collection. With imports from 15 countries, he features an impressive collection of tin mirrors from Mexico, some mighty fine hand-tooled leather goods by Alexis David, lamps, attractive metal wall pieces, including evocative wire sculptures by Raymond Wiger, along with a few pieces of interesting furniture and plenty of things to check out and crave.

Plaid

715 8th Street, SE
Washington, DC 20003
202-675-6900
www.plaidstore.com
Tues-Sat: 12-7, Sun 12-5

Owner Sarah Chellgren opened Plaid in October 2003 with the goal of providing designer clothing at reasonable prices. There is lots of cute stuff here: Glenda Gies bags and Bedhead sleepwear were my favorites. If you are young or slight, there's some fine apparel that is just up your alley. And, if you are too busy to shop during regular hours, Plaid will host a party for you and your friends, with munchies, so you can take your own sweet time.

What's to Eat?

Starfish Cafe
539 8th Street, SE (corner of 8th and E Streets)
202-546-5006 • www.starfishcafedc.com
Lunch, dinner, Sunday brunch

Delicious seafood served in attractive surroundings.

Banana Café and Piano Bar
500 8th Street, SE
202-543-5906
Lunch, dinner, Sunday brunch

Puerto Rican, Latin American, Cuban, and Tex Mex—it's all tasty.

14th & U Streets

This is a community with a rich and turbulent history. Back in the late 60's the area was decimated by riots, and the once-thriving businesses disappeared. Today, it's a happening neighborhood, thanks to serious revitalization and an active business owner's association. There are two good things about this area: one, all of the stores are small businesses owned by folks who took a leap of faith and followed their dreams (in some cases, literally!), and two, all the owners know each other and are working together with the neighborhood residents to make their community thrive.

go mama go

1809 14th Street, NW
Washington, DC 20009
202-299-0850
www.gomamago.com
Tues-Sat: 11-7, Sun: 12-5, Mon: 12-7

What's big and orange and invites you in? go mama go. Once you get in, you notice the huge aluminum and neon tree in the front window. Then a small display with a fountain, then, along the side wall, there's a large frame filled with black. Most people walk by without looking or stopping and ask, "Why is that black thing hanging there?" But if you pause and look into the center of the blackness, a tree emerges. Creepy and cool. This work of art may be gone when you visit, but I'm confident that another just as striking will take its place.

go mama go is filled with fun and interesting tableware—especially Japanese dishes, gift items, and art of all sorts from all over. I particularly liked the metal bras on the back wall, but we won't go into that. It's an eclectic mix of things you love and can imagine using.

Noi Chudnoff, owner and definitely a "going" person, joined Home Rule (below) on the block just six weeks before September 11, 2001—not the best time for retailers or anyone else. After pouring thousands of dollars into renovating the rundown thrift store, she didn't think she would make it. But, the gay community came out that October and bought big ticket items to make sure she got on her feet and could pay her rent. Today, she's settled in, and helping the community that has helped her make that successful move from her former location—a 10 x 10 tent in Eastern Market.

Home Rule
1807 14th Street, NW
Washington, DC 20009
202-797-5544
www.homerule.com
Mon-Sat: 11-7, Sun: 12-5

In 1999, Rod Glover and Greg Link had a concept for a store featuring current housewares, but retail rents were too high everywhere they looked. So, they did what great entrepreneurs do: they looked for a new area with potential. This led them to a boarded-up building that had once been a machine shop on 14th near U Street. And in this building, they carved out their dream.

Of course, this story has a happy ending, because from the first day, Home Rule has been a success, as well as a leader in the revitalization of an area of our nation's capital that had been long neglected. As Rod sees it, 14th Street is the middle of the city, not the edge, and is accessible from all over the metro area. The street and sidewalks are broad and invite a stroll.

Home Rule is a bright, compact space, chock-full of kitchenware, accessories for you, your bath, and your home, along with special things you need for entertaining. There are lots of colorful, fun utensils that can make the mundane chores of life more exciting, like a striped floor mop or a roll of paper towels with green feet. There's lively glassware for your favorite beverages, along with innovative products for making the most of your parties. I especially liked the clips that hold your wine glass to your plate, so you can eat and drink simultaneously without support. Their collection of trash cans is great, and you can even buy a sparkly shower curtain to add a certain thrill to those necessary ablutions.

The Garden District
1801 14th Street, NW
Washington, DC 20009
202-797-9005
www.gardendistrict.biz
Mon-Fri: 10-7, Sat: 9-7, Sun: 11-5

Right on the corner is a lovely little oasis amid the concrete with plants, pots, benches, and a helpful, enthusiastic staff. If you love gardens, and only have space for a pot or two, this is the place to buy great ones and the flowers to fill them. If you have more space, say, several acres, all the better!

What's to eat?

Ben's Chili Bowl
1213 U Street, NW
202-667-0909 • www.benschilibowl.com
Breakfast (except Sunday), lunch, dinner

Just three blocks away, you can eat at a Washington landmark, Ben's Chili Bowl. No frills, but great chili dogs and French fries since 1958. Or you can go early and have one of their famous breakfasts and get ready to shop, shop, shop!

Pulp
1803 14th Street, NW
Washington, DC 20009
202-462-7857
www.pulpdc.com
Mon-Sat: 11-7, Sun: 12-5

Pulp on the Hill
303 Pennsylvania Avenue, SE
Washington, DC 20005
202-543-1924
Mon-Sat: 11-7, Sun: 12-5

Come Feel the Love! Then, come feel it again and again, because this store requires more than one visit! When you enter this magical two-level space, it's hard to know what to love first! Take it all in. A riot of color! Greeting cards—sweet, irreverent, sassy, slightly obscene; magnets displayed on an old Kelvinator; wrapping paper and ribbons; journals for small or big thoughts; candles for every mood; pens of every color; calendars; books, especially historical books on the surrounding neighborhoods. There's also a card bar where you can sit and write your greeting cards on the spot.

Opened by Ron Henderson in April 2003, Pulp is a joyous store, owned by a joyful man who loves his work and his customers. The first time I visited, it was hot and he was passing out cold bottled water. Everyone enjoys being in this space, but beware, it's hard to resist pulling out that credit card. And apparently, Pulp is popular, because Ron has opened an equally wonderful location right on Capitol Hill. (Now, that's a place that definitely needs to feel some love, don't you think?)

No matter where you shop, be sure to add your name and birthday to the mailing list. They'll send you a card and give you a 10% discount. I asked for something twisted and sick. Can't wait to see what I get!

Nana
1534 U Street, NW
Washington, DC 20009
202-667-6955
www.nanadc.com
Tues-Sat: 12-7, Sun: 12-5

Who can resist the little store that Jackie Flanagan named for her grandmother? Look for the colorful clothes painted on the building, and come on into this homage to a woman who was her "fashion icon." Jackie believes that everyone should be able to dress well for reasonable prices, so her store stocks "new and almost new styles for the savvy shopper." It's sort of a trip down memory lane with prints and polyesters from the 60's and 70's. She also carries a line that features vintage fabrics re-cut into current styles. Funky handbags, hats, personal care products, and candles—Nana is definitely a proud grandma!

Millennium Decorative Arts

1528 U Street, NW
Washington, DC 20009
202-483-1218
www.millenniumdecorativearts.com
Thurs-Sun: 12-7

Continue that look back in Millennium—a store for the decorative arts of the 60's, 70's, and 80's. If you remember avocado, harvest gold, and all those groovy accessories, it'll be deja vu all over again.

Zawadi

1524 U Street, NW (first floor)
Washington, DC 20009
202-232-2214
www.zawadigallery.com
Mon-Sat: 11:30-7, Sun: 12-5

Irene Whalen opened Zawadi in 1992—a pioneer on this block. She specializes in African art and artifacts and textiles, personal accessories, art objects, and home furnishings, along with African American documents and memorabilia. But that doesn't quite describe this sweet-smelling shop that gives us the chance to appreciate the creativity of another continent's peoples and cultures. My favorite object was from Cameroon—a huge red feather hat worthy of a princess or a special place on your wall at home.

Meeps

1520 U Street, NW
Washington, DC 20009
202-265-6546
www.meepsonu.com
Tues-Wed: 4-7, Thurs-Sat: 12-7, Sun: 1-6

Vintage clothing for women (and men). Look for the 7-way Wonder Dress (circa 1973 updated for the 21st century) and cool stuff made of vintage polyester fabrics. Also ask about wedding dresses and try on some interesting eyeglass throwbacks.

Wild Women Wear Red

1512 U Street, NW
Washington, DC 20009
202-387-5700
www.wildwomenwearred.com
Mon-Sat: 11-7, Sun: 11-5

One night, while serving in the Peace Corps in Namibia, Toddre Monier had a dream that she opened a shoe store named Wild Women Wear Red. She came back to Washington and met her husband, Bill Johnson, who, coincidentally, had a similar idea, but had never acted on it. So together they created Wild Women Wear Red, a funky, functional shoe boutique that opened in 2002.

Though small, the store's space is maximized by the custom fixtures and seating designed by Bill, a gifted metal worker and furniture designer.

(His studio, at 4627 9th Street, NW, is open by appointment, call 202-829-1059.) That superb fit and craftsmanship extends to the footwear.

The shoes are definitely not mainstream, but neither are they extreme. Made in soft leather with reasonable heels in riotous colors and patterns, the majority of the selections are handmade by small manufacturers, like Kemper, XOXO, and United Nude. If your feet were made for walking, then these shoes will make you light on your feet because they are so much fun. There are also colorful handmade hats and some beautifully crafted one-of-a-kind clothing—both new and vintage.

You never know what you will find at Wild Women Wear Red, but once you've discovered the wild woman in you, there will be no turning back.

What's to eat?

Lovecafé
1501 U Street, NW
202-588-7100 • www.cakelove.com
Breakfast, lunch and open late into the evening

If you get tired, pop across the street and taste the artistry of lawyer-turned-baker Warren Brown. When his bakery, Cakelove (1506 U Street), proved to be such a success, he opened a little café just across the street that features individual servings of the desserts we've come to love. Have a delicious cup of coffee and munch on a slice of the made-from-scratch cake—sandwiches, too!

Georgetown

In 1751, just two years after Alexandria was founded across the Potomac, Georgetown began its life in a similar fashion—as a commercial port. Originally a part of Maryland, it was annexed to the nation's capital in 1871, and became known as a fashionable quarter of the city. Back in the late 60's, it was the hub of the hippie movement, and a great place to hang out (you could drink at 18 then). Its stores were innovative and new, and Georgetown was a place to stroll, eat, and shop. But, when the neighborhood declined a Metro stop, it lost some of its cachet, and in the years since many of the wonderful, innovative shops and restaurants have closed and been replaced by chain stores. However, there are some definite gems here, and Georgetown is still one of the area's major shopping neighborhoods.

Pirjo

1044 Wisconsin Avenue, NW
Washington, DC 20007
202-337-1390
Mon-Sat: 10-7

4821 Bethesda Avenue
Bethesda, MD 20814
301-986-1870
Mon-Fri: 10-6

My friend Ann is probably the most daring, stylish dresser I know. Of course, she buys the best she can afford and it never goes out of style, so Pirjo, naturally, is one of her favorite shops.

Located just over the canal on lower Wisconsin Avenue, this little store has been in its current location since 1989. The owner, Pirjo Jaffe, has a love of those American and European designers that specialize in what I call an "any-age" look: beautiful, natural fabrics, wonderful workmanship, and interesting asymmetrical, sometimes flowing, designs. There is Marimeko clothing—don't mistake it for the fabric—and Rundholtz bags. Just about anyone can find something that works, but when you see it on someone who wears it well, like my friend Ann, it inspires envy.

Dream Dresser
1042 Wisconsin Avenue, NW
Washington, DC 20007
202-625-0373
www.dreamdresser.com
Mon-Sat: 11-8

Talk about a contrast! Right next door to Pirjo is Dream Dresser. The window display might give you a hint, but inside you'll find all kinds of things that are meant to inspire passion, or release it. There are spike heels you have to practice to wear, thigh-high boots, whips, "gear" (collars, cuffs), sex toys, and an incredible line of clothing from girlish to down and dirty! The corsets are fabulous and there was a rhinestone bra I admired, while my friend Jennifer liked the fishnet stockings. I was surprised to learn that this is the only place in town where you can get a rubber nurse's dress or cat suit. And, I understand that you can polish it so it looks just like your skin. There's even an inflatable bondage bed complete with straps.

"...the only place in town where you can get a rubber nurse's dress..."

The shop has been around since 1992, but only in this location since 2000. There is a sister store in West Hollywood, California (where else?). If you can't find the attire you desire, they can order it for you in any size, or you can go to their website. If you need a date for the weekend, there are a few accessories that might tickle your fancy.

A Mano
1677 Wisconsin Avenue, NW
Washington, DC 20007
202-298-7200
Mon-Sat: 12-6, Sun: 12-5

If you've ever visited Deruta, Italy, you'll recognize many items in this little shop just up Wisconsin Avenue. A Mano not only carries handmade Italian and French pottery, but also English crystal, hand-blown Simon Pierce glassware, and sumptuous table linens. It's the perfect place for brides to register because they have everything anyone might need to achieve "the art of the tabletop."

Since 1996, A Mano has catered to those who love fine things. Jeff Kazmarek, manager of the store, says most of his clients are well-traveled and understand the value of fine tableware. They often come to A Mano to relive the memories of trips they've enjoyed, and perhaps buy that one piece they didn't want to carry home in their luggage. A Mano also has a large selection of ceramic pots and other garden accessories. And, there is a big half-price table that is hard to resist.

New items come in every week, but major containers arrive four times a year. The store takes special orders and maintains a bridal registry, and a visit to the website will give you a good idea of what's available. A Mano has another store in Naples, Florida.

Rooms with a View

1661 Wisconsin Avenue, NW
Washington, DC 20007
202-625-0610
www.roomswithaviewdc.com
Mon-Sat:10:30-6, Sun: 12-5
  (closed Sun/Mon in summer)

Just down the hill from A Mano is another "by-hand" type of store, but this time it's fine papers and writing accessories and lots more. Jill Mahoney has amassed quite a collection of note cards, invitations, gift bags (with beads!), diaries, pocket-sized journals, specialty books for parties, tote bags, notepads, and ribbons of all sorts during her 12 years in business. While she carries popular mainstream lines of stationery, like Meri Meri and Mari-Mi, she also has an excellent selection of paper goods made by individual artisans she discovers at small juried fairs in the United States and Europe. I bought a friend a memo cube with pencil holder that says, "Tomorrow is the future and yesterday is the past and today is a gift— that's why it is called the present."

*Also in Georgetown, see **The Written Word** (listed in Dupont Circle).*

Dupont Circle

Right in the middle of Dupont Circle, one of those wild and crazy circles Washington is famous for, is the Dupont Memorial Fountain, designed by Daniel Chester French, sculptor of Lincoln's statue in the Lincoln Memorial. Years ago, it was another great hippie hangout. Today, it's a lovely part of our city that's been reborn in the last quarter century. It's a great walking neighborhood with glorious row houses and a few remaining 19th century mansions.

The Written Word

1365 Connecticut Avenue, NW
Washington, DC 20036
202-223-1400, 888-755-4640
202-463-7484 (fax)
www.writtenword.invitations.com
www.writtenwordstudio.com
Mon-Fri: 10-6, Sat: 11-5

Canal Square	*Berkeley Springs, WV*
1054 31st St., NW	*21 N. Washington St.*
Washington, DC 20007	*Berkeley Springs, WV 25411*
202-342-1033	*304-258-0883*

I just love stationery stores, and The Written Word is one of the best. This store is specialized—you can't get imprinted napkins or matchbooks, but you can get exquisite invitations, top-quality paper, a full selection of imprintables, and, best of all, custom-designed, letterpress-printed announcements and invitations.

Paul and Marti Rubenstein bought The Written Word in 1980. You can really see the care and attention they've put into gathering a wonderful inventory that includes the traditional Crane and William Arthur lines, edgy imprintables by Roger de la Borde, diaphanous Midori ribbon, wrapping paper, and selected greeting cards, blank journals, mix–and–match loose paper, and business paper for resumes and other correspondence.

"...what sets The Written Word apart from other stationery and paper stores is the antique letterpress..."

But, what sets The Written Word apart from other stationery and paper stores is the antique letterpress (1885) they use to create 21st century designs. (Letterpress is just the opposite of engraving and thermography.) If you have a concept for a party, the staff—all capable designers—can work with you to convey your look and message, and then beautifully print it at their Berkeley Springs location in just four weeks. (If you visit there, you can see the letterpress in action!)

But, don't worry, they also use the latest in printing technology to produce customized invitations and other stationery gift products, such as stickers, business cards, and notepads in much less time.

They also have the ability to take those imprintables that you select from their shelves and save you the trouble of doing them yourself.

Can't get to one of their three locations? The website is well-organized with a full range of products, including imaging, photo cards, and photo frames.

Second Story Books

2000 P Street, NW
Washington, DC 20036
202-659-8884
www.secondstorybooks.com
Daily: 10-10

4836 Bethesda Avenue
Bethesda, MD
20814
301-565-0170

12160 Parklawn Drive
Rockville, MD
20852
301-770-0477

Have you ever noticed how many books there are out there? Like new cars, they quickly become used, but they never rust away. Alan Stypeck has made a great business out of used, second-hand, or previously owned books—whatever you want to call them.

While a student at American University, Alan did a small mail-order business for out-of-print books, but he soon needed to expand, which he did, into a store on Connecticut Avenue. And as time went on and the number of new books becoming used books increased, he eventually had six locations. He's refined his physical locations to three, but Second Story Books has an active website and a booming ebay business.

What types of books, you ask? All types. He buys from individuals and estates and at auctions. He has well over one million books in stock. The Dupont Circle store has that Dickensian feeling and smell. Don't expect to run in and out—you'll find yourself stopping to peruse the antique prints, and fondle the old LP's, and reminisce about the used videos and CD's. Then, maybe, you'll start with the bookshelves. If you are in a hurry, go to the website, which is friendly and gives lots of search options and alerts you to deals and new collections, and imparts interesting book facts.

If you just inherited a library from your old Uncle Morty and some of the books look suspiciously valuable, you can always contact Alan for an honest and professional appraisal. He teaches book and manuscript appraising at The George Washington University, is a senior member of the American Society of Appraisers and just about every other antique book society in the country, and also does a weekly show on NPR—The Book Guys—that takes call-in questions.

I don't care what anyone says, if you have a book, you'll always have a friend—Second Story Books is a great place to make friends for life.

Toast and Strawberries

1608 20th Street, NW
Washington, DC 20009
202-234-1212
www.toastandstrawberries.com
Mon-Fri: 11:30-7, Sat-Sun: 1-6

Talk about a trip down memory lane. When I was a hippie college student, I shopped at Toast and Strawberries. It had opened in 1967, but I don't think I found it until about a year later. Whenever I was home on break, I made the trek to Dupont Circle to see what was in. Toast and Strawberries is just as cool as ever and it's still owned by Rosemary Reed Miller, who has spent the last 37 years immersed in her community and fashion.

Toast and Strawberries is a small store in an old row house, but it holds lots of good things. As you browse through her racks of clothing, look for new and local designers like Christopher Williams and Donna Baptiste. There are some interesting consignments, as well as trendy and funky jewelry from Mark Baker Lovett and many other designers. Sizes range from small to extra-large, and alterations are available. They even have things that will work as bridesmaids' dresses.

Rosemary believes that her shop is a community resource, so she often features shows for new designers, book signings for local authors, fundraisers, and other neighborhood events. One Monday every month, she hosts a networking evening where business owners from around the metro area can meet, greet, exchange business cards, and share their stories while generating business. Also, Rosemary has just published her own book: *Threads of Time: The Fabric of History, Profiles of African American Dressmakers and Designers from 1860 to the Present.* Toast and Strawberries has just about everything—except toast and strawberries!

What's to eat?

Teaism
2009 R Street, NW
202-667-3827 • www.teasim.com
Breakfast, lunch, dinner, Sunday and Saturday brunch

Simple elegance infused with relaxed informality, this funky Asian teahouse is a neighborhood jewel. It offers a charming selection of simple dishes, from ginger scones to Bento boxes and savory curries, at reasonable prices.

Adams Morgan

This is the city's hot spot. With its multicultural crowd, vibrant night life, and ethnic eateries, Adams Morgan is more an entertainment arena than a shopping place. But, there are some little shopping places that cater to that hip generation, and you can bop in before you go to dinner and then dancing.

Daisy
1814 Adams Mill Road, NW
Washington, DC 20009
202-797-1777
www.daisyclothing.com
Mon-Sat: 12-8, Sun: 12-6

Daisy Too and Zelaya
4940 St. Elmo Avenue
Bethesda, MD 20814
301-656-2280
Mon-Sat: 10-6 (Thurs until 8)
  Sun: 12-5

Daisy, a "unique girlie boutique," sits on a corner and just looks like fun. It's fun for young women of a certain age, and I liked looking around keeping my friends and their young daughters in mind. Daisy specializes in trendy, fashionable clothing created by youthful, up-and-coming designers. Among their many selections are Michael Stars T-shirts that are soft and colorful (one size fits most), Ruth dresses that are darling, kicky little Ella Moss skirts, and the moderately-priced Free People line. They also have Paper Denim Jeans which are all the rage, and Tarina Tarantino accessories. The Bethesda location has a separate shoe boutique, Zelaya, to keep you current from head to toe.

A Little Shop of Flowers
1812 Adams Mill Road, NW
Washington, DC 20009
202-387-7255
www.dcnet.com/littleshop
Mon-Sat: 9-7, Sun: 12-5

This is not your ordinary florist. Owner Sefika Kurt and her staff specialize in pretty, fresh, and unusual flowers and plants. You will not find a carnation in the place, but you will find mature Money Trees (Pachira), Agapanthus by the stem, and an unusual variety of Protea. The arrangements are natural and colorful, with interesting mixes of flowers.

Even if you don't need any flowers or a houseplant, stop in and just breathe deeply. It smells great and you'll get a sensory lift that will improve your day.

All About Jane
2438 18th Street, NW
Washington, DC 20009
202-797-9710
www.allaboutjane.net
Mon-Sat: 12-9, Sun: 12-7

2839 Clarendon Boulevard
Arlington, VA 22201
703-243-4424
Mon-Sat: 11-9, Sun: 12-6

You can't write a book about shopping without mentioning All About Jane. A trendsetter in Adams Morgan, All About Jane opened in the year 2000. Kathy Atkinson, the owner and trendwatcher, was a buyer for Nordstrom in a previous life, until she set out on her own with her vision of what girls wear.

Jane is "the girl next door…who thinks traditional dressing is boring. She loves adventure, independence, friends, and family. She wants to be sexy and have fun." Sound like anyone you know? If so, she probably knows about All About Jane and does her shopping there. And she looks good in the latest denim from hot young designers, plus lots of color and 60's- and 70's-style wrap dresses and wild prints.

All About Jane is a great shop for that self-assured young woman who sees dressing as not only fun, but a personal statement.

Foxhall Square

It's a medical building. No, it's a mall. Wait—it's both! Tucked away just off New Mexico Avenue, Foxhall Square is an intimate and interesting shopping experience. And, you don't have to be sick to enjoy it!

Tree Top Toys

3301 New Mexico Avenue, NW
Washington, DC 20016
202-244-3500
www.treetopkids.com
Mon-Sat: 9:30-5:30

Langley Shopping Center
1382 Chain Bridge Road
McLean VA 22101
703-356-1400
Mon-Sat: 9:30-6, Sun 11-4

When I was a kid, a Tiny Tears doll was about the coolest thing, along with Tinker Toys and Mr. Potato Head. Today's kids are much, much luckier, I guess, except they have SO many choices. That's the only problem with Tree Top Toys…and clothes and books.

Tinker Toys now are rivaled by Pixel Blocks that are translucent, ZOOB Modeling Systems, and Coin Construction that lets you use your spare change to make something.

There's an entire line of medieval soldiers and knights, made by Ritter in Germany (take that, Mr. Potato Head!), along with lots of girlie accoutrements, like Hello Kitty. Of course, Radio Flyer wagons and wheelbarrows are represented, along with lots of those connect-the-dot books. I really didn't see too much I could recall from my childhood, but there was something like a Hula Hoop called a Beamo. I did find a desk accessory for my husband: a rocket pen that flew and sat on its very own launch pad. He was thrilled.

There's a very large selection of books—you name it, they have it. I asked a young man what age range the books covered, and he said he was 21 and could always find a classic that interested him. They have story hours with readings by local authors, and a tea party was an upcoming event. The McLean location has a story hour every Sunday at 2:00.

Across the hall, Tree Top Toys has a small shop that carries infant and toddler clothing and gifts. Gift wrapping is free (I used green frogs for my husband's present). If you can't get in, visit the website; it's user-friendly and toys are grouped by season.

Abrielle
3301 New Mexico Avenue, NW
Washington, DC 20016
202-364-6118
Mon-Sat: 10-5:30

Lest you have never experienced 400+ count bedsheets, you've missed one of life's best luxuries. Add fluffy towels and gorgeous sleepwear, and you really will think you are a princess. All these things, and lots more, are available in a profusion of colors and designs at Abrielle.

Owner Ann Sullivan came up with Abrielle while studying for her MBA. The assignment was to analyze a business and the professor suggested a utility company. But what self-respecting woman would be interested in gas when linens could make you just as comfy. So, Ann and two classmates presented the idea of creating and analyzing a lingerie store. The trio got an A and that was that.

Several years later, Ann and one of her classmates decided to make that class project a reality and opened Abrielle in 1986. Using her knowledge of the textile world, Ann has gathered a wide range of suppliers from Italy and France that produce a virtually unlimited number of luxurious items for your bath, your bed, or your table, as well as for your children, your guests, and yourself. Maria Scotto nightgowns, cashmere pajamas, Gordensbury hand-embroidered baby clothes, Signoria 400+ sheets in a multitude of colors, chenille throws, guest towels, and handkerchiefs. A bed displaying just a few of the lovely selections beckons.

There are also beautiful linens for your table in sizes perfect for an intimate dinner for two or a state banquet. Ann can supply seamless tablecloths up to 102 inches wide and any length. She also has sources that can restore old or damaged linens.

Abrielle also carries accessories, such as wastebaskets, along with the popular Thymes, Riguad, and Votivo lotions, candles, and soaps. I left the store with a small gift for a gentleman (gift wrap is free), and went home and ironed my sheets. You'd be surprised how much better I slept!

Pamela Barkley
3301 New Mexico Avenue, NW
Washington, DC 20016
202-363-3569
Mon-Sat: 9:30-5:30, Sun: closed

My friend Joan remembered Pamela Barkley from her time on Capitol Hill about 25 years ago. Now, the shop has expanded into two facing locations in Foxhall Square: one for clothing, the other for gifts. The ladies clothing selection includes some excellent handmade sweaters from the United States, Canada, and Europe, Blue Willi's denim that's soft and comfy, Garfield and

Marks jackets, and a small selection of Mycrapac microfiber raincoats with handbags. Accessories run the gamut--the small, hand-painted tin purse was quite intriguing. The shop does trunk shows four or five times a year, which allow customers to meet their favorite designers.

The gift store has a large selection of Vera Bradley, some useful tableware, and some aromatic Red Flower candles—the jasmine scent was very appealing. Pamela Barkley is a good place to visit whenever you need a calming shopping experience.

Be aware: during the week, the first hour of garage parking at Foxhall Square is free, but the fees are pretty steep after that hour and no one validates. Parking is free on Saturday.

Cleveland Park

Designed as a streetcar suburb in 1894, Cleveland Park has a remarkable collection of Victorian homes, plus a few big estates, like Marjorie Merriweather Post's Hillwood (worth a visit!). President Grover Cleveland summered in Cleveland Park, hence its name. In the block across the street from the Uptown Theatre—one of the last period movie houses in the city—you'll find some interesting and useful shopping stops.

Wake Up Little Susie
3409 Connecticut Avenue, NW
Washington DC 20008
202-244-0700
Mon-Fri: 11-7, Sat: 11-6, Sun: 12-5

Wake Up Little Susie is full of lots of things from the ridiculous to the sublime for just about anyone in your life, from young to old—like a pig catapult with refills!

Owner Susan Linn started her retail career at Jordon Marsh in Boston, but woke up (ha, ha) and opened her own vintage clothing store on Capitol Hill in 1977. In 1988, she moved to Adams Morgan and then to her current location in 1993, where she is a well-established neighborhood fixture, and an oft-mentioned source of all things trendy. Her retail philosophy: "Sell all the stuff I like!"

"If you ever think your goose is cooked, drop into Wake Up Little Susie and say ooh, la, la!"

We seem to like the same stuff because everything in Wake Up Little Susie is appealing to me—and lots of other folks. Color, color, color in the form of handmade jewelry (cement earrings!), trendy gadgets, games, cards, soaps, and cutting-edge wearables. It's one of my favorite places for favors, gag gifts, or hostess gifts. The next baby gift I buy will be a romper that says, "Been there, done nothing." If you ever think your goose is cooked, drop into Wake Up Little Susie and say ooh, la, la!

Artisan Lamp Company
3331 Connecticut Avenue, NW
Washington, DC 20008
202-244-8900
Mon-Sat: 9-6:30

If you find an old lamp that looks bad, but has potential, don't dismiss it. The Artisan Lamp Company can repair, rewire, or restyle it so it can have a second chance. Since 1979, John Teymouran and Cyrus Manaf have salvaged and repaired vintage and antique lighting, and will work with you to buy, sell, or trade something you have for something you want. Their collection of chandeliers and table lamps, along with antique tables and side chests and a few paintings and mirrors requires a serious browse. If you have any lampshades that have turned to dust or your cat has chewed up, they can recover them, as well. In today's throwaway society, isn't it nice to find a place that can restore the past and give it a new future? Check it out!

Friendship Heights

I have always liked the name of this area. It spans the District and Maryland on the west side of Connecticut Avenue. It has a Metro stop, a dense concentration of high-end chain stores, plus the Mazza Gallerie. You can find some real gems amongst the big time retailers.

The Point of It All
5232 44th Street, NW
Washington, DC 20015
202-966-9898
Mon-Fri: 10-5:30, Sat: 10-4

Celebrating 30-plus glorious years, The Point of It All is going strong. Maybe it's the color! Hundreds of hand-painted canvases just waiting to be covered with colorful thread hang all over the red, red walls. Or maybe this little shop's biggest strength is its owner, Hyla Hurley, who has built this business and its loyal clientele with her innovative stock and bubbling personality. As my friend Peggy says, "As a stitcher, Hyla's makes me very excited!"

Even if you're not a stitcher, you can still have fun. Come on in and check out the wide variety of wise and wiseacre pillow canvases: "If you look like your passport photo, you probably need the trip." Or an old Mae West standard: "Men are like linoleum. If you lay them right, you can walk on them for 30 years." Other favorites are "And they lived happily ever after" and the Ruby Slippers.

There are projects big and small from furniture, rugs, and handbags to eyeglass cases and shoes and belts and Christmas ornaments. If Hyla doesn't have something that you want, she has hundreds of artists who can create a canvas to your specifications. She can teach you how to stitch and if you don't want to learn, she has people who will do it for you. (She does sell her samples if you are into instant gratification.)

To fill all those little holes, you need supplies. It's difficult to describe the choices of yarns and fibers to choose from: silk, velvet, wool, sparkly, plain, and every color in the spectrum. The canvas may be painted one color, but you can use any color you want. And the staff is ready to help you select exactly what and how much you will need.

Now, once you've filled in all those holes, you must turn that well-handled canvas into a work of art. That's another one of Hyla's strengths. When she's finished, you have a treasure that can be used and admired for generations. Every First Lady starting with Rosalyn Carter has received a finished needlepoint picture of the White House courtesy of the Point of It All. Barbara Bush was a loyal customer during her years in Washington. If you kiss Caddie, the resident Coton de Tuelar (fuzzy white dog), you've narrowed your degree of separation down to two with lots of famous people.

Needlepoint may not be for everyone, but it's an art that has endured for centuries. Let's hope the Point of It All does, too.

Finials

3813 Livingston Street, NW
Washington, DC 20015
202-362-8400
Tues-Sat: 11-5, Sun: 12-5

Finials embodies its definition: a finishing touch or flourish. I absolutely cannot think of one thing in the world that does not improve with embellishment, and Finials is filled with lots of options. Opened in 1999 by Debbie Burg, Barbara Lautman, and Nancy Plotsky, this little shop just off Connecticut Avenue has both old and new items that will fit anywhere you need a little accent. As the sign directs: "Never stop to think, 'Do I have a place for it?'" The owners gather their stock at auctions, yard sales, and other foraging opportunities, and have come up with an ever-changing assortment of "stuff" that will enrich your surroundings or those of your friends: little paintings and drawings, crystal, silver, old signs, architectural finds, lamps, furniture—all items are sold "as is."

> *"I absolutely cannot think of one thing in the world that does not improve with embellishment..."*

When I visited with my friends, Robyn and Melissa (who both found some treasures), I found a sign I thought I would give to my neighbor for his birthday. It says, "Eat, be merry, drink." My philosophy exactly!

Periwinkle, Inc.

3815 Livingstone Street, NW
Washington, DC 20015
202-364-3076
Mon-Sat: 10-6, Sat: 12-5

Right next door is Periwinkle, a store that fills lots of needs and creates lots of wants. It's bright, sunny, and has a big, big variety of things to buy and buy. Pottery, frames, calendars, note cards, lotions and potions, candles, and, best of all, candy, candy, candy. Owner Judy Philactos got her start with Dean and DeLuca and has spent the last seven years (the first three in her basement) finding wonderful gifts and, that all-time favorite, great homemade and imported chocolates and other candies. In the back, there is a whole case of treats, including Blue Moon chocolates (made in Bethesda), Laderach, B.T. McElrath, and Hammonds (from Colorado). If you like licorice, she has some of the very best from Jelly Belly.

Judy does gift baskets, but my idea of the perfect gift from Periwinkle would be a gift certificate. That way, you can indulge yourself in any way you choose. Maybe a little parsley hand lotion and a box of bonbons. True decadence.

Catch Can

5516 Connecticut Avenue, NW
Washington, DC 20015
202-686-5316
Mon-Fri: 10-5 (Thurs until 8), Sat: 10-6,
   Sun: 11-5

1050 Metropolitan Avenue
Kensington, MD 20895
301-933-7862
Mon-Sat: 10-5, Sun: 12-5

My friend Robyn introduced me to Catch Can a couple of years ago. Obviously I had been deprived because it's been in its Connecticut Avenue location since 1992. Robyn likes Catch Can because the clothing is "forgiving" (i.e., comfortable, unfussy, and natural). Susanne McLean, an at-home mom, started selling leather baby booties by mail order out of her basement in 1983. She built up a loyal clientele and catered to "hippie" mothers. Then, when people started knocking on her doors and disturbing her children's naps, she opened a children's store in Kensington in 1989, and the rest is history.

The Connecticut Avenue store is staffed by many artists and sells clothing (Andrea Lieu, Willow, Flax, Cut-Loose, Yasuko are top lines), handmade jewelry, Merrill and Dansko shoes, great socks, wild peepers (for our aging eyes), and wonderful housewares, furniture, and accessories. The Kensington store has all that, plus giftware and an extensive children's line.

Museum Shops

There are at least 30 major museums in the Washington area—17 of them are part of the Smithsonian Institution. All have gift shops, and there's some great shopping to be had! Here are three good bets.

The Arthur M. Sackler Gallery of Art

1050 Independence Avenue, SW
Washington, DC 20013
202-633-0535
www.freersacklershop.com
Daily: 10-5:30

This is an extraordinary shop with all things Asian. Besides the requisite books and jewelry, there are beautiful embroidered wool jackets from Kashmir, a wide array of incense, lovely textiles for your table, origami paper, tea things, Tibetan painted chests, and lots, lots more. This museum is connected to the Smithsonian's Freer Gallery of Art (Jefferson Drive at 12th Street, SW), which also has a smaller selection of similar merchandise. Both of these shops, unlike the other Smithsonian shops, buy independently, and it shows! Oh, don't forget to stop and take a look at Whistler's Peacock Room and the beautiful screens while you're there.

The National Building Museum
401 F Street, NW
Washington, DC 20001
202-2772-7706
www.nbm.org
Mon-Sat: 10-5, Sun: 11-5

If you are around the MCI Center, the National Building Museum is just a short walk away. Before you go in, stop and admire the lovely structure, designed in 1881 and completed in 1887. The frieze that encircles it depicts a parade of Civil War military units. Once inside, the Great Hall is well worth a pause for its graceful fountain, massive Corinthian columns and tiers of open arches encircling the hall for several stories. (The website has a virtual tour.)

The gift shop is much more intimate, however, and chock full of items to buy. Dr. Skud Fly Swatters, mobiles, magnets, an eclectic collection of household and garden items. As you might expect, the book section includes many titles about all buildings, great and small, and ideas for your home and garden. The wide selection of accessories (men's ties, interesting key rings, watches designed by noted architects, such as Maya Lin), posters, prints, kid's stuff to stimulate your budding I.M. Pei, as well as ornaments of the Pentagon and the World Trade Center, makes this museum shop a real find. You can also shop at this store online.

The Museum of Women in the Arts

1250 New York Avenue, NW
Washington, DC 20005-3970
202-783-5000
www.nmwa.org
Mon-Sat: 10-5, Sun: 12-5

While many of these items and their creators are scattered in other shops around the city, this is sort of a one-stop shop, and, as you would expect, a haven for women's creativity. There are red feather hats, Oui Bee watches, jewelry from designers like Lisa Jenks and Judith Jack, textiles from Sara Schneidman, and numerous books written by and about women. If you want something to inspire a young girl, *Girls Think of Everything* is a good choice. The gift shop is accessible without paying the entrance fee, but don't miss the opportunity to check out the exhibits before or after you shop.

Gotta Shop!

maryland

Bethesda

What can you say about Bethesda? The sprawling suburb northwest of Washington seems to have no boundaries; it goes from Chevy Chase, across the beltway and up to Interstate 270. It's a serious mix of old and new homes, quiet streets and traffic jams, several country clubs and notable research and medical facilities. And just like the suburb, Bethesda shopping defies categorization. It's just as wide and varied as the area itself—definitely worth exploring.

Montgomery Farm Woman's Cooperative Market

7155 Wisconsin Avenue
(Between Willow and Leland Streets)
301-652-2291
Wed and Sat: 7 a.m.–3 p.m. year-round

This little unassuming green and white frame building has been the home of the Bethesda Farm Woman's Cooperative Market since 1932. Farm women in Home Demonstration Clubs of the Extension Service at the University of Maryland launched this venture as a hedge against the Depression, falling prices, and drought. And, despite setbacks, it has continued to be an unchanging resource in a community that is constantly changing.

The big hand-painted sign reads: Produce, Meat, Poultry, Fresh and Dried Flowers, Prepared

Food, Fine Teas, Eggs, Seafood, Baked Goods, Plants, Herbs, Art, Crafts, Jewelry, Aromatherapy (I'm sure that was added recently). It's all there, supplied by 26 individual vendors. Mid-winter Wednesdays are quieter than usual, but there's always activity, time for a chat, and things to admire or buy. On my last visit, I bought my first bunch of daffodils, and admired some beautiful estate jewelry. There was fresh bread, hot food, some handmade jewelry, and even an optical stand where you could buy some funky eyeglass frames and have a prescription filled.

On beautiful Saturdays, vendors spill out into the surrounding yard. On Sundays, from 8 to 5, there's a flea market with 50 dealers (www.bethesdafleamarket.com).

Three Dog Bakery
4924 Elm Street
Bethesda, MD 20814
301-654-1540
www.threedog.com
Mon-Fri: 10-7, Sat: 10-6, Sun: 12-5

OK, there are 23 other Three Dog Bakery stores scattered around the country—the closest to us is located in New York—but the store is a pet lovers experience where dogs are allowed. The canine treats are made by the on-site pastry chef, who uses human-grade ingredients, but no butter, sugar, or salt. (Sounds like diet food to me!) The pastries and cakes are so appetizing that I had to have a nibble of one of the treats I bought for my Chocolate Lab friend India. Alas, they looked much prettier than they tasted (like most diet food!). Unfortunately, before India got her treat, my cats had grabbed them from my purse and eaten them. If you are planning a special pet celebration, Three Dog Bakery does custom orders and ships cakes to any location.

Once you get past the bakery cases, there is a real fire hydrant surrounded by pet requirements of all types. It's a dog lover's paradise! And I think my cats might like it, too.

WHAT'S TO EAT?

Green Papaya
4922 Elm Street
301-654-8986
Lunch, dinner (Sunday dinner only)

Stop by for terrific Vietnamese food, and indoor and outdoor dining.

Bethesda–Chevy Chase

Back in the 1890's, two gold and silver magnates, Francis Newlands and William Stewart, bought thousands of acres of land just north of the capital and built a town called Chevy Chase. It took a while to catch on, but the streetcar and then the automobile made living "out of town" a reasonable alternative. Now, Chevy Chase is "in town" and business is booming.

Sylene

4407 South Park Avenue
Chevy Chase, MD 20815
301-654-0494
www.sylene.com
Mon-Sat: 10-6

Did you ever wonder why Mona Lisa is smiling? I'm convinced it's because she was wearing a lacy bra and underpants from the 16th century version of Sylene.

Just off Wisconsin Avenue on the border of Friendship Heights and Chevy Chase, you'll find Sylene. Owned by two sisters, Helen Kestler and Cyla Weiner, who grew up in the lingerie business, Sylene offers three decades of experience in the art of undergarments.

Every woman has the opportunity (and the responsibility) to be fitted for the perfect bra to enhance her figure and ensure her comfort. That's where Sylene comes in with their full-service approach to intimate apparel. With many imported makes—Casabella and La Perla from Italy, Le Mystere and Chantal from France—their extensive inventory guarantees that you will find something to make you feel special, regardless of your shape or size. The selection of sleepwear and loungewear is broad, and bathing suits for all body types are a year-round specialty. Sylene sponsors swimwear trunk shows several times a year, and customers can order anything straight from the designer.

For brides, there's a registry and an amazing array of items from bikini panties with "Just Married" in sequins across the bottom to full-scale white night gowns and robes. Plus bridesmaids, or anyone for that matter, needing just the right foundation garment for those strapless dresses that are all the rage, will find exactly what's needed to keep everything in place.

Men are welcome to shop anytime, but they have their own special afternoons during the holidays and around Valentine's Day.

But the most marvelous service at Sylene is the special attention given to women who have undergone all types of breast surgery. Not only do they hold fundraisers for women's health non-profits, like Gilda's Club, they sponsor breast prosthesis trade-ins for women's shelters, and provide fittings and prostheses for low-income women.

Bethesda-Wildwood Shopping Center

Several friends kept saying, "You need to go to Wildwood Shopping Center!" So, my wonderful friend Rachel and I headed out on an adventure one sunny day. I remember this row of stores, on Old Georgetown Road at Democracy Boulevard, from years ago, and even visiting the Sutton Place Gourmet, but I never realized what else was right under my nose! While there are some darling clothing stores like Sequel, a branch of South Moon Under, along with home furnishings like the Kellogg Collection, and the usual bank, hairdresser, spa, and other necessities of life, there are two stores worth a special trip.

Red Orchard

10217 Old Georgetown Road
Bethesda, MD 10814
301-571-7333
Mon-Sat: 10-6 (Thurs until 8)

John Helm and Caroline Liberty started out selling library furnishings in Vermont. In 2002, they moved into whole-house crafts and into our area, bringing with them an exquisite sampling of furniture, glass, metal, and more—all handcrafted in Vermont (and a few things that slipped over the border).

Begin your visit by admiring the focal point of the store—a 75-piece ceramic tree made by

Marly Miller. Pet the five-foot, hand-carved and hand-painted pine dog by Norton LaTournelle. Buy a metal magnet made by Payne Junker and try on a chapeau by Susan Bradford. If you really like shopping, there are some wonderful glass shopping bags (from Canada). The furniture is what you might expect from the Guild of Vermont Furniture Makers: stunning wood, natural finishes, simple designs—all custom made. Red Orchard also carries Studio Z Mendocino stationery for the invitationally challenged. (OK, it's from California, but it's really fun stuff.)

Warm, open, and natural, Red Orchard is serene and comfortable, and a joyous place to spend some time.

ZYZYX

10301A Old Georgetown Road
Bethesda, MD 20814
301-493-0297
www.zyzyxonline.com
Mon-Fri: 10-6 (Thurs until 8),
Sat: 10-6, Sun: 12-5

Three things about ZYZYX: First, it's pronounced like physics with a z. Second, it's named for a road off of Route 15 between Los Angeles and Las Vegas (they have a photo of the sign). And, third, the manager is a man named Joyce, who, as he says, is the most unusual thing in the store.

Named as one of the Top 100 Niche Retailers in American Crafts, ZYZYX is an ACC (American Crafts Council) shop that has handmade works of 2,500 artists from around the country—many of them local. Now, I know there are a lot of shops around the area that feature American crafts, but there's just something about this one. While they don't sell clothing, they have jewelry aplenty. Some of the things I liked the best were the ceramic plaques ("Spank your inner child and get on with it"), and the decorative mirrors that will make you smile no matter how bad you may look in the morning. They have Judaica, including lots of attractive Mezuzahs for your doorposts. The glasswork demonstrates the highest level of artistry, as does the metal sculpture. Both media are well represented and worth a second look.

> *"... it makes you believe in the creativity of American craftsmanship."*

If you can't make it to the ACC Show that comes to Baltimore every year, you can always drop by ZYZYX any time. When you look at the wealth of beautiful objects, it makes you believe in the creativity of American craftsmanship.

What's to Eat?

Geppetto Café
10257 Old Georgetown Road
301-493-9230
Lunch, dinner

Delicious Italian food—the pizzas are excellent, the service is good, and the prices are right.

*For more stores in Bethesda, see listings in the District of Columbia for **Pirjo** (Georgetown), **Second Story Books** (Dupont Circle), and **Daisy** (Adams Morgan). Also, see the listing in Virginia for **Bruce's Variety Stores** (Alexandria-Hollin Hall).*

Wheaton

Describe Wheaton in one word: eclectic. My friend Rolfe lives in Wheaton and he very graciously squired me around the Wheaton Triangle—the area surrounded by Viers Mill Road, Georgia Avenue, and University Boulevard. Because of Wheaton's diverse population, the triangle has an incredible stash of unusual shopping opportunities.

Barry's Magic Shop, Ltd.
11234 Georgia Avenue
Wheaton, MD 20902
301-933-0373
www.barrysmagicshop.com
Tues-Sat: 11-6

Don't go to Barry's Magic Shop unless you are ready to be astounded and amazed. Barry Taylor and his lovely wife, Susan, along with their wonder dog, Frankie, are a magical trio, and can make you magical, too!

Barry, who has been a performing magician since he was 12, opened his magic shop 30 years ago. He stocks books, videos, and DVDs, along with a vast array of magical implements for beginners to hobbyists to professionals. He has top hats, wands, scarves, costumes, fire sticks—paraphernalia big and small that will help you learn a trick or two. (I didn't see any live rabbits, but I bet he could get them for you.) You can even get the gear to saw your better half in half.

If you want to learn a few cocktail party tricks, Barry has books but recommends a DVD or video, because what used to take two paragraphs to explain now takes just seconds to illustrate from a variety of angles. Barry is always happy to demonstrate card tricks, sleight of hand, or any other little trick you may be interested in learning, and Susan, who is equally adept, has a particular attachment to the resident ghost, Glorpy. Both of them are available to astound and amaze your next party guests if you, like me, have no talent for illusion (www.barrytaylor.com). I don't believe they'll bring Frankie, the best doggie soccer goalie in the world, but he will demonstrate his prowess if you ask.

Barry, whose Psychic Ghost Theatre production was a Helen Hayes nominee several years ago, is out of the theater business now, but continues to sponsor an open magic night every other Thursday, which features up-and-coming magicians of all types. You might get a look at the next David Copperfield! Or, you can just come in on a Saturday when would-be Houdinis come in to soak up Barry's advice and encouragement.

I spoke to a gentleman in the shop who told me he took up magic when the first of his six grandchildren was born. He was back for a visit with two of his pre-teen granddaughters, who grew up with an amazing granddad and now were eager to learn some tricks for themselves. Barry's Magic Shop—let's hope it never disappears.

Bonifant Books

11240 Georgia Avenue
Wheaton, MD 20902
301-946-1526
Mon-Fri: 10-8, Sat: 10-6, Sun: 11-6

Just down the street, pop into Bonifant Books for used books of all sorts. It's well organized, well-lit, not too dusty, and has good prices.

The Jewish Bookstore of Greater Washington

11252 Georgia Avenue
Wheaton, MD 20902
301-942-2237
Sun: 10-5, Mon-Wed: 10-6, Thurs: 10-7,
  Fri: 10-2, closed Sat and Jewish holidays

You don't have to be Jewish to love this Jewish Bookstore and its neon sign in the window "If It's Jewish We Have It." This is not false advertising.

Joshua Youlous founded the store 31 years ago and has been building his inventory ever since. The father is joined by his son, Menachem, and his wife, Eva (who calls herself the holy ghost), in a labor of love.

Torah cards, prayer shawls in all fabrics (including denim), Bibles, maps, books, music, and menorahs crowd the two-room shop. Mr. Youlous is proud that he has something for everyone and says that at least 30 percent of his customers are non-Jewish. He carries seven-branch candelabras for Christmas along with extensive Bible study aids.

But the most unusual items in this shop are its Torah scrolls. The family works to recover scrolls from around the world that were stolen or hidden during World War II, and restores them for sale. Menachem specializes in the restoration and uses special inks and quill pens to return these holy documents to places of worship.

If you are in the area, stop into The Jewish Bookstore of Greater Washington. It's a place for everyone of any faith.

Barbarian
11242 Triangle Lane
Wheaton, MD 20902
301-946-4184
Wed-Fri: Noon-6:30, Sat: Noon-5, Sun: 1-5

For an incredible collection of comics, games, and nostalgia, go right next door to Barbarian. Check out the life-size ET and ask to meet

Flaming Carrot Man—the superhero who fights his enemies with a broken bottle and a Pez dispenser. WOW!

The Little Bitts Shop
11244 Triangle Lane
Wheaton, MD 20902
301-933-2733
Tues-Thurs: 10-7, Wed-Fri: 10-6, Sat: 9-5

This amazing little shop is a mecca for cake decorators, candy makers, and party givers. Founded by Margie Bittenger in her garage, it has been in this location in Wheaton since 1975, and the domain of Bob and Ann Schilke since 1988.

From character cake pans (think Sponge Bob), baking cups, and little paper umbrellas to two entire walls of candy molds, this place has everything. For example, you can fill the life-sized 3-D squirrel mold with chocolate or concrete! Fill that couch potato mold with chocolate or glycerin soap! Or just buy the chocolate and you can mold a set of sweet dentures any dentist would love. And, if you can't find the mold you really need, they can get a custom one made just for you.

Of course, a big part of their business is weddings. Amateurs and professionals from all over the area come to Little Bitts to take advantage of their endless supply of stands, columns, pans, flowers, and innumerable decorating tools. Their selection of those little brides and grooms comes in all races and combinations, and the same sex toppers are on the way!

Ann, a Wheaton native, runs the shop, while her husband, Bob, teaches a full schedule of evening and weekend classes. Aspiring bakers from all around the metro area flock to learn Basic and Advanced Cake Decorating, hone their skills at specialty classes like Butter Cream Flowers and Gingerbread House Construction, and enjoy candy demonstrations.

Did you know that plumbers use peppermint oil to detect pipe leaks? Well, they buy it in bulk at Little Bits. So, even if you lack a culinary clue, the Little Bitts Shop has something just for you!

Showcase Aquarium

11250 Triangle Lane
Wheaton, MD 20902
301-942-6464
Mon-Sat: 10-7, Sun: 12-6

Showcase is dark (sunlight encourages algae growth) and steamy (all that water). But look at it this way, a visit to Showcase is not only interesting and fun, thanks to all that humidity, it also does wonders for the complexion, as evidenced by Kathy, daughter of owner Joe Myers.

Like many successful business owners, Kathy says her dad started small—breeding guppies. In 1968, he opened Showcase Aquarium and began the fascinating work of creating both freshwater and saltwater aquatic wonderlands for hobbyists and businesses in the area. Today, the shop is filled with incredible fish and a few reptiles that all want to come and live with you.

So, say you want to start a fish neighborhood, Kathy can get you started with an aquarium from one-half gallon to 210 gallons (bigger is better because of less maintenance) or an outdoor pond up to 600 gallons (dig your own hole, please). Once you decide on fresh or salt water, you need the basic utilities—pump and filter system, heater, chemicals, lights—and then decorations—gravel, varieties of aquatic plants and coral, fanciful structures, shells, and other little hiding places, just in case you have some modest fish. Then you get to pick who lives there. Of course, the staff at Showcase can point you to the best combination of fish to avoid the aquatic equivalent of the Hatfields and McCoys.

And what choices they have! Not just goldfish (did you know they can live from 30-40 years?), but also Blue Arrowana, Kissing Gormies, Angelfish, Swordtails, Tetras, along with Koi (they can live for 100 years and eat out of your hand) and even a Teacup Stingray. Saltwater fish are more colorful than freshwater, but the combinations are myriad.

Creating and maintaining an aquarium is just like having a pet. And just as you can hire a dog walker, Showcase can provide tank maintenance and will test the water quality for free. They also have gift

"...the shop is filled with incredible fish and a few reptiles that all want to come and live with you."

certificates and monthly sales on specific tanks and setups, so if you think an aquarium might be in your future, the best place to start is Showcase.

The Toy Exchange
11265 Triangle Lane
Wheaton, MD 20902
301-929-0690
Mon-Sat: 11-7, Sun: 12-5

This is a multi-generational boy toy store and a great place for a father to take his son (or daughter). For 12 years, the Toy Exchange has specialized in old toys, trains, and collectibles. Slot cars and Hot Wheels are parked on the ceiling, while memorable action figures from Star Wars to James Bond and Davy Crockett are displayed in cases. One wall is dominated by Lionel, American Flyer, and Marx vintage trains, some of them dating back to 1903. The store is also an authorized Lionel Value-Added dealer and service station.

But the owner's real passion is his collection of robots. Whether you want an original or a replica, it's a good bet that Perry Mohney will have it for you. My husband is a total space cadet (and I mean that in the nicest way!), and he said it was the best collection of robots he had ever seen. In fact, he walked out with two of them (something else to dust!)

Shalom Strictly Kosher Market

2307 University Boulevard West
Wheaton, MD 20902
301-946-6500
Sun: 8-6, Mon-Weds: 8-7, Thurs: 8-8, Fri: 8-3

Around the corner, look for the Shalom Strictly Kosher Market. Owned by the Dekelbaum family, this market has great meats and baked goods produced under rabbinical supervision. And there is an adjoining deli if you need a nosh.

Takoma Park

Old Town Takoma Park is a terrific place to spend a day just wandering around. Carroll Avenue is the main drag, where people are friendly, shops are plentiful, and tasty food abounds. While you're there, take a drive through the area and admire the beautiful homes—many with front porches and verdant gardens. It's obvious that residents love their community.

House of Musical Traditions
7040 Carroll Avenue
Takoma Park, MD 20912
301-270-9090
Tues-Sat: 11-7, Sun-Mon: 11-5

"Folk Instruments, Books and Recordings from Around the World, Lessons, Concerts, Repairs, Imports and Mail Order Sales Since 1967." Koombyah! The House of Musical Traditions specializes in acoustic instruments of all types. It's a great place to hang around and just look at the drums—big, small, African, beat, snare, bass—you name it, they have it. They have a whole room devoted to guitars. There's sheet music galore, harmonicas, and five different types of kazoos, not to mention whistles. I bought a nose flute to astound and amaze my friends, which it did! If you are into heavy metal, this probably isn't the music store for you, but it inspires beautiful music just the same.

Finewares

7042 Carroll Avenue
Takoma Park, MD 20912
301-270-3138
Tues-Fri: 12-7, Sat: 11-6, Sun: 12-5

Finewares is a lovely two-floor space filled with the work of East Coast artists. In business for 22 years, Finewares probably has the best selection of innovative and traditional pottery in the Washington area. It also has jewelry, sculpture, glass, and paintings. It's a great place to browse, and the prices range from very reasonable to investment level. There are so many things worth coveting—and a short visit will stimulate your creative senses.

Polly Sue's Vintage Shop

6915 Laurel Avenue
Takoma Park, MD 20912
301-270-5511
Mon-Fri: 11-7, Sat: 11-6, Sun: 11-5

Polly and Susan just loved old clothes and accessories, so they united to open Polly Sue's, a divine shop full of all things old. Of course, the 60's and 70's are considered old today, so some of these things may seem like just yesterday to those of a certain age. These ladies shop at estate sales, auctions, and yard sales to find relics of our past. Evening wear is their specialty, and they actually have bridal gowns (remember when brides wore high necks and sleeves?). I found a fabulous pair of aluminum eyeglass frames with swoops, and the hats collection may bring back afternoon tea. Teens will love those bellbottoms and little peasant blouses. I just kept asking myself why I didn't save all those tent dresses and platform shoes!

What's to eat?

Savory
7071 Carroll Avenue
301-270-2233
Breakfast, lunch, dinner

My friend Louise and I enjoyed the home-style cooking.

Summer Delights
6939 Laurel Avenue
301-891-2880
Seasonal

Enjoy a cone of homemade ice cream.

Hyattsville

Like many small towns around the metro area, Hyattsville began with the railroad. Named after Christopher Clarke Hyatt, the town was incorporated in 1886, and, conforming to the wishes of Mr. Hyatt, the city charter forbade the sale of alcoholic beverages within the city limits. Glad that charter has been amended.

Franklin's

5123 Baltimore Avenue
Hyattsville, MD 20781
301-927-2740
Sun-Mon: 11-9, Tues: 11-9:30,
   Weds-Thurs: 11-10, Fri-Sat: 11-11

You can't miss it: "Shop, Eat, Enjoy" in blazing neon. You just have to stop. Franklin's combines two of America's favorite things: shopping and eating. In an 1880's landmark building on Route 1 that once housed a blacksmith and carriage shop, Franklin's was the Hyattsville Hardware Company from 1910 to 1992, when it became Franklin's General Store.

Using many of the original hardware fixtures, including the nail bins, Mike Franklin has managed to amass an inventory that includes something for everyone. I couldn't locate a whoopee cushion, but that's because I was so enthralled by the squishy balls filled with worms and the shelf of imported chocolates and the idea of a Dashboard Jesus. Mainstream gift ideas and comestibles include an excellent selection of wine, gourmet foods, and a full collection of hot sauces, candles, bath soaps, and greeting cards. Two young moms with their infants were thrilled with the wide selection of age-appropriate toys and games their children could grow up with.

At Franklin's, you have a choice: eat and drink first and then shop, or shop and then eat and drink. You win either way. In 2002, a brewpub ("the best little pourhouse in Maryland") and restaurant were added next to the general store. Of course, there is a wide selection of handmade brews, but also some pretty good brewpub food in generous portions. General manager Larry Wise says more additions are coming—so keep eating and shop often.

Mt. Rainier

Since its establishment in the late 19th century, Mt. Rainier has seen its fortunes rise and fall like so many other communities surrounding Washington, D.C. I remember my grandmother taking me to visit my great, great-aunt Eva when she lived there in the 1950's. Aunt Eva was a remarkable woman, fit and active well into old age, and very health conscious. She grew beautiful roses and drank vinegar and honey every morning before doing her exercises.

GLUT Food Co-op
*4005 34th Street (One block north of
   Rhode Island Avenue)
Mt. Rainier, MD 20712
301-779-1978
www.glut.org
Tues-Fri: 9-8, Sat-Mon: 9-7*

I bet Aunt Eva would have liked GLUT. And she would have liked all the people who have kept it going since 1969. GLUT began in a church basement in Georgetown, the center of the hippie movement in Washington. In 1971, it moved to its current Mt. Rainier location as the hub of the area's pre-order food co-ops that were the rage during the 60's and 70's. The group started selling what was left over on the weekends, until a full-time store was established. Today, the non-profit collective grosses more than $2.2 million annually in its 2,000 square-foot space.

Since its founding, GLUT has been run by consensus. There are 16 cooperative members who work in the store. Lynn Terrell, one of the 16 members and an opera singer, says that their volunteers "really keep us afloat." She should know because she started out as a volunteer 15 years ago, working one shift a week and earning products worth up to $600 annually. Today, she manages the frozen food section.

While each section has a manager, there are no bosses at GLUT. Chris Doyle, one of the leaders of the cooperative, is a carpenter by trade and an avid supporter of Mt. Rainier. He said this little enclave on the northeast side of the city is really the only true Bohemian neighborhood left. It is populated by liberals who work for non-profits or in the arts, the housing is still affordable, and there is a real "sense of place." The store itself smells great—warm and comfortable. And since it was a grocery store for over 70 years, it's a perfect location for GLUT.

When it was founded, GLUT basically wanted to flood the market with cheap food. And the prices are still great on a wide range of natural foods, juices, and products for just about everything. They carry lots of loose herbs and teas, so you only have to buy what you need (and avoid paying for McCormick packaging). You'll find fresh products from Tuscarora Farms, New Morning Farms, and Trickling Springs Dairy. While 90 percent of the grains are organic, they have lots of conventionally grown produce and other natural foods, as well as the familiar Firehook Bakery breads. My friend Karen and I shared an absolutely delicious homemade carrot muffin in lieu of lunch. I got Haas avocados for a buck a piece. The "virtuous" (politically correct) foods, such as the fairly traded coffees and teas, are very appealing, as are the herbal rubs, soaps, bath products, and natural remedies for everything from arthritis to constipation to lung congestion.

You can even buy organic seeds for your garden.

If I lived in the neighborhood, I'd do all of my grocery shopping at GLUT. But, since I don't, I think I'll join all the other people who come from as far as Baltimore to buy their favorite products.

Nisey's Boutique
4007 34th Street
Mt. Rainier, MD 20712
301-277-7977
Wed-Fri, Sun: 12-6, Sat: 10-6

Nisey Jackson is a real woman, "not like Oprah," she says. She's proud to be married to a Washington, D.C. policeman ("He gets the husband of the year award!"), the mother of five children, a member of the PTA, and a small business owner with an incredible spirit and a joy that permeates her lively boutique.

A Washington, D.C. native, Nisey opened her shop in 1998. She married into a family with a lot of retail experience, and she has used that knowledge to build a business that appeals to just about everyone. While she does have Afrocentric items like Dashikis and hats and personal care products, Nisey prides herself on being creative and mainstream in her selections. It was very hard to resist the attractive, reasonably priced array of straw hats, and there were some wonderful burnt velvet capes to dress up the little black dress. She carries Urban Oxide bags, and current little items like rhinestone initials to hang on your cell phone.

And Oprah doesn't have anything on Nisey, because she has the complete line of Carol's Daughter lotions and potions. They are all natural, smell terrific, and began life in Carol's basement and grew to be featured on Oprah. Nisey also carries Nubian Heritage soaps, Black

Earth, and Zum products. There are also some collectibles available, like the limited edition Venus and Serena Williams dolls. She also has books, postcards, and selected musical instruments (a man bought a drum from Mali during my visit).

Personal service is serious business and Nisey has a way of making you feel important; within an instant, every customer is a friend. And an added bonus: if it's not too busy and Sylvia, proprietor of Serenity Space, is there, you might just get a free three minute seated massage. Sylvia, who operates her therapeutic massage business in Nisey's lower level area, has several services to choose from, and if three minutes is a good sample, I can't imagine how great you would feel after an hour. (You can reach Sylvia at 202-297-0224.)

Oxon Hill

Oxon Hill is not a place that comes to mind when you think about going shopping. Straddling the Beltway, the Prince George's County suburb is on the fence: not quite city, not quite country. And in this unlikely place you'll find a gem!

Desserts by Gerard

6341 Livingstone Road
Oxon Hill, MD 20745
301-839-2185
301-839-9300 (fax)
Tues-Sat: 6:30-6:30

How many ways can you say "Yummy"? Let's count the Desserts by Gerard! And then we can add the breads, the soups, the sandwiches, the croissants…

Tucked away in a forlorn shopping center, surrounded by a nail salon and a beauty supply store, Desserts by Gerard could be overlooked. But, it isn't. That's because once you've sampled the work of Gerard Huet, you tend to tell all your friends, and then they tell their friends, and so on. I heard about this bakery from my friend Ann, who regularly bought pastries for office parties and other soirees. I then told my friends at work, and we started going to Gerard's for his great sandwiches and soups.

With his wife, Katherine, Gerard opened the bakery in 1990, after honing his skills at the Jean Louis Restaurant at the Watergate Hotel, in Beverly Hills, in Miami, and in France. His creativity is evident when you stand before the cases filled with mini-pastries, tarts of all types, cheesecakes, quick breads, cakes, cookies, and Gerard Missu (his own version of the popular

Italian classic). Everywhere you turn, there is something delectable. With two weeks notice, Gerard also does catering and wedding cakes.

It must be very hard to work in Desserts by Gerard. But, when I asked Kay, an employee of 10 years, she said it wasn't hard at all for her since she was selling such a great product. She said she had tasted everything, and, of course, I asked her about favorites. She said, "Everything is great—the strawberry shortcake, the cheesecakes, the croissants. How can you choose?" I choose those Pecan Thingys (that's what they are called!), but you have to stop by and give everything a try.

Thurmont

WORTH THE TRIP—*If you aren't lucky enough to have a helicopter, it's about a 60-mile schlep up to Thurmont, which is just past Frederick, Md., and home to Camp David. You probably couldn't tell that the sleepy little town of Thurmont is the center of the goldfish growing industry. At the foot of the Catoctin Mountains, Thurmont is very close to Cunningham Falls State Park, and some great camping and hiking. But you really don't have to be a government VIP, a fish lover, or tree hugger to visit Thurmont.*

Discount Fabrics
108 North Carroll Street
Thurmont, MD 21788
301-271-2266
www.discountfabricsusa.com
Mon-Sun: 10-6

It's worth a trip to Discount Fabrics if you are in need of some decorative changes. In the 10 or so trips I've made for myself and with friends, there's always something new to see, and at rock bottom prices.

This cavernous warehouse is filled to the ceiling with rolls and rolls of top quality fabric for upholstery, draperies, pillows, curtains, tablecloths, shower curtains—you name it. You'll find every color, every weave, leather, suede, outdoor, sheer, silk, cotton, polyester, retro designs, classic tapestries, toile, and many of the designer fabrics featured in home magazines. There are remnant tables where everything goes for half price, if you buy the rest of the roll. In the back, fabrics are sorted by color. If you want something at the top of the pile, you can climb a ladder to get a closer look and feel, before you ask the kind gentlemen to bring the forklift and bring the pallet down. Sometimes it takes a few determined women to extricate the desired roll from the piles at floor level, and it's not uncommon to share opinions and suggestions with your fellow shoppers.

In the past two years, Discount Fabrics has added an extensive collection of trims to finish off your project. It's hard to resist the beaded trims and tassels of every color and size. It's a temple to embellishment. When you finally settle on your purchases, and the team of knowledgeable ladies cuts and wraps your rolls, be sure to add your name to the mailing list—Discount Fabrics has several sales during the year that really make it worth the trip. Also, you can visit the website where they feature high-end fabrics from around the world at significant price reductions.

What's to Eat?

The Tasting Room
101 N. Market Street
240-379-7772
Lunch, dinner (Reservations suggested)

You definitely need lunch before or after a visit to Discount Fabrics. If you want a really fine experience, try to make it back to Frederick, to a small, stylish, innovative restaurant with the best lobster chowder ever, an extensive wine list, terrific martinis, and fabulous desserts. Believe me, it's worth a stop.

Davidsonville

WORTH THE TRIP—*Amid the fields and pastures of Anne Arundel County, Davidsonville is not much more than a zip code just this side of Annapolis, Maryland's state capital. It really is a most excellent destination for a drive into the countryside to celebrate nature.*

Homestead Gardens
743 W. Central Avenue
Davidsonville, MD 21035
410-798-5000, 301-261-4550
www.homesteadgardens.com
Mon-Fri: 9-8, Sat: 8-8, Sun: 9-6

Ever wondered what the Garden of Eden would look like in the 21st century? I think it would be like Homestead Gardens. No one runs around naked, but there are lots of temptations!

Founded in 1973 by Don Riddle, Jr., this family-owned business has grown to be the second-largest single location garden center in the country (and is rapidly reaching first). But, Homestead is not just big, it's also beautiful year-round, and that's because of the talented employees who make any visit a rewarding experience.

Any good gardener will tell you that a nursery is only as good as the quality of its plants and service. Homestead grows all of its plants, except tropicals, on-site on its two, 100-acre farms or in its five-acre enclosed greenhouse. If the plant isn't healthy, it's gone. The staff—numbering 300 at the peak of the season—is well-informed and many are trained horticulturists. They can answer any question you have about what, how, and where to grow anything.

Homestead has a year-round events calendar with something happening every month: the Spring Flower Show (think mini-Philly), the Fall Festival in October (hay rides and lots of activities for kids), and a huge Holiday open house (cutting-edge displays created by staff designers Scott Daly and Ann Ketchem, along with unique ornaments and decorations). But the activity doesn't stop when January rolls around. Every gloomy winter weekend brings a seminar that will help keep those winter doldrums away: feng shui for gardens, building hypertufa troughs, making grapevine wreaths, care for lawns, the art of bonsai—the list goes on. You can even learn to knit or make a felted tote— thanks to the resident llamas and their fibers.

Of course, there are garden clubs for all ages, but if you don't like getting your hands dirty, there is an extensive selection of silk flowers, garden-themed gifts, and gorgeous indoor/outdoor furniture and all the attendant accoutrements required for an elegant lifestyle. Can't decide? You can have your landscape designed and planted by their excellent crew, and if you are lucky enough to have your own personal gardener, there's a wholesale operation, as well.

Homestead Gardens was founded with love, is run with care, and really lives up to its slogan: "Because Life Should Be Beautiful." Ahhhhh.

Tropic Bay Water Gardens
200 W. Central Avenue
Davidsonville, MD 21035
410-798-1800
Mon-Sat: 10-6, Sun: 10-5
(Hours are shorter in winter, longer in summer)

Stephen Koza started water gardening as a hobby years ago: "I wasted a lot of money and killed a lot of fish." So, instead of giving up, he learned from his mistakes, studied the business and opened Tropic Bay Water Gardens in 2001 to help people have their water gardens without making his mistakes.

It is obvious that Stephen has done his homework. He has absolutely everything you need for a water garden: liners, pumps, landscape decorations, plants, and lots and lots of fish, including Koi of all sizes. The setting is quite lovely and he's made numerous displays, both inside and outside, to illustrate the many possibilities, both large and small. If you don't want to do anything on a major scale, he has a lovely selection of indoor fountains and fog machines—which I just craved—along with lots of pots and other garden ornaments.

If you don't want to install your own pond, he works with three contractors, who will do it for you and do the landscaping, to boot. Stephen can also provide any maintenance service you may need throughout the year. I'm starting to think that a nice pond with some trickling water is just what everyone should have to relieve stress. And Tropic Bay Water Gardens can make it stress free for you.

What's to eat?

Killarney House
584 W. Central Avenue
410-798-8700 • www.killarney-house.com
Lunch, dinner, Sunday brunch

Just what the name implies, tasty Irish dishes—fish and chips, lamb stew, corned beef and cabbage—in a pleasant setting with good service and reasonable prices. They also have American items. I had a terrific Reuben on one of my visits, and from what I hear, the liver and onions are great. They also have hamburgers, salads, and crab cakes, so you don't have to be Irish to eat at Killarney House.

Gotta Shop!

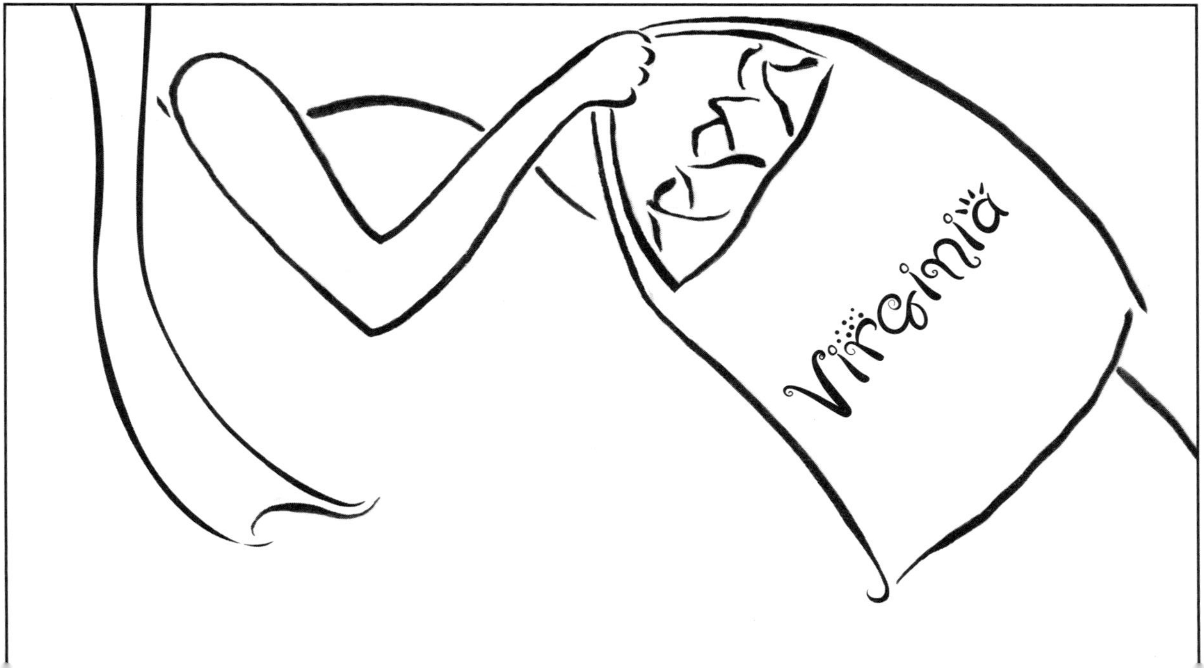
Virginia

Alexandria—Old Town

In 1749, a group of merchants decided that they needed a place to sell their wares, so they established the settlement of Alexandria along the Potomac River with Market Square right in the center. George Washington shopped here—he slept down the road at Mount Vernon among other places—so I guess that makes Alexandria the granddaddy of America's shopping malls.

Today, thanks to the King Street Metro and reasonable evening parking in city lots, Old Town Alexandria has the same attraction that Georgetown had back in the 70's. The number of shops is astounding and there are so many that are innovative and fun, that a stroll down King Street or on any of its side streets puts any kind of shopper, window or otherwise, in a place close to heaven.

The Alexandria Farmers' Market

301 King Street (Market Square)
Alexandria, VA 22314
Sat: 5-10 a.m., year-round

Still located in Market Square, surrounding the fountain in front of City Hall, the Alexandria Farmers' Market is the oldest, continuously operating, open-air market in the United States. You'd be surprised how many familiar faces, famous or otherwise, you run into from 6 until 10 a.m. on a Saturday morning. I met Katie Couric one morning, and there's always a local politician around. You also meet lots of pleasant and helpful vendors from Maryland, Virginia, Pennsylvania, and West Virginia, who sell fresh vegetables, baked goods, plants, and flowers. Local artisans also sell handmade clothing, pottery, jewelry, and other artsy/craftsy items. Virginia residents can register to vote, and anyone can bring sick plants or mysterious leaves to the free plant clinic sponsored by the Northern Virginia Master Gardeners. Pickings are slim in the dead of winter, but in the spring, summer, and fall—especially around the holidays—you're likely to find lots of tasty and colorful shopping.

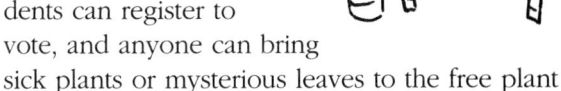

What's to eat?

You can buy coffee or delicious baked goods, including REAL ham biscuits, from a variety of vendors and sit by the fountain (it comes on at 8 a.m. with a gasp from the crowd) and watch your fellow shoppers.

The Torpedo Factory Arts Center
105 King Street
Alexandria, Virginia 22314
703-838-4565
www.torpedofactory.org
Daily: 10-5

The Torpedo Factory Arts Center is right on the river at the corner of King and Union Streets. This building, one of several, was built in 1918 to manufacture torpedoes, but closed just after World War II. The buildings were used for Federal Government storage until 1969, when the City of Alexandria purchased them. The City wanted to raze the buildings until it was discovered that the buildings were built to withstand torpedo explosions (duh!), so they were renovated instead. With lots of community support, perseverance, and good taste (thanks, Marian Van Landingham!), the Torpedo Factory Arts Center opened in 1974 as an artists' enclave.

Today, more than 160 artists and craftspeople, who have passed the jury process, work and sell their creations in 83 studios and six galleries. All media are represented: painting, photography, fiber arts, metalsmithing, jewelry, sculpture, and ceramics. The studios, all with large windows, line a three-story center space that lets you window shop with abandon. There's nothing cheesy here and it's worth some time to experience the creative energy that bounces off the walls. The small art-themed gift area at the entrance has quirky gifts, books, and toys.

"an artists' enclave"

If you are artistically inclined yourself, The Art League of Alexandria also has an extensive educational staff, program of classes and workshops, and a well-stocked art-supply store on the second floor, where you can buy what you need to create your own works of art.

Why Not?
200 King Street
Alexandria, VA 22314
703-548-4420
Mon: 10-5:30, Tues-Sat: 10-9, Sun: 12-5

A couple of blocks from Market Square at the corner of King and Lee Streets is a great little shop for kids—Why Not?. Erin, a friend and mother of two extraordinary little girls, loves Why Not? for its great toys and educational games. And, best of all, she testified, "They gift wrap for free!"

This cheerful little shop is a veritable paradise for children and all those who love them. Two floors chock full of games, books, play or special occasion clothing, and other accoutrements just for kids of any age. I've never seen so many hair ribbons! In 2003, this great establishment celebrated its 40th anniversary—a one-of-a-kind success. The staff is pleasant and knowledgeable, and best of all, the first floor has a small toy-filled enclosure where toddlers can play while moms browse nearby. So, if you are in the market for something special for any child or anyone's inner child, why not shop at Why Not?.

La Cuisine—The Cook's Resource
323 Cameron Street
Alexandria, VA 22314
703-836-4435, 800-521-1176
www.lacuisineus.com
Mon, Tues, Wed, Fri: 10-7, Thurs: 10-7,
  Sat: 10-6

This is a gem of a store. Nancy Purves Pollard has made sure, since 1971, that La Cuisine has lived up to its name—The Cook's Resource. La Cuisine is a cozy place. Not overwhelming like the chain kitchen stores, but chock full of interesting and esoteric "must haves" for any kitchen. It's a place to go to buy copper pots that will last a lifetime or a zester that really works. No trendy gadgets here, just innovative, high-quality tools and products for the professional and home cooks.

Each item Nancy stocks is carefully and independently selected, and because she buys directly from suppliers around the globe, La Cuisine's prices are very competitive. Several years ago, I needed candied violets, and I found them at La Cuisine for the best price. The line of shelf-stable food items is quite alluring and diverse.

La Cuisine publishes a lively quarterly newsletter, "A La Carte," which has 20,000 subscribers and is available by mail or online. And the website also features menus, complete with shopping lists, from the large selection of in-stock cookbooks. Add worldwide shipping to all of this, and La Cuisine is a resource you can share with your friends.

Gossipya
325 Cameron Street
Alexandria, VA 22314
703-836-6969
www.gossypia.com
Mon-Sat: 10-6, Thurs: 11-7, Sun: 12-5

While you're in the neighborhood, take a peek in Gossipya for clothing for every occasion—some casual, some dressy. There's even a selection of wedding dresses that are perfect for an informal, outdoor, or second time around celebration.

Elder Crafters of Alexandria, Inc.
405 Cameron Street
Alexandria, VA 22314
703-683-4338
www.eldercrafters.com
Tues-Sat: 10-5, Sun: 1-5

There's one more great little place in the heart of Old Town that my friend P.K. really likes and that's Elder Crafters. This shop sits quietly on the corner of Cameron and Royal Streets and is completely filled with items made by nearly 200 crafters ages 55 and older from 21 states.

Established in 1982, the non-profit endeavor relies on consignments and the work of volunteers to keep things going. Elder Crafters only accepts well-made, top quality items, so you will find some handsome quilts and afghans, beautifully stitched children's clothing, innovative toy and gift items, and professional-level woodworking and ceramics. Elder Crafters keeps a portion of every sale for their intergenerational enrichment and instruction programs. The stock is always changing, so it's a great place to visit whenever you are in the area.

Alexandria—W.O.W. on King Street

Wander up King Street, west of Washington Street—W.O.W.—toward the King Street Metro station, and you're guaranteed to find something new every time. This area has blossomed in the last couple of years, and the variety of stores and eateries are worth a special visit.

Ten Thousand Villages
824 King Street
Alexandria, VA 22314
703-684-1435
www.tenthousandvillages.org
Mon-Weds: 11-7, Thurs-Sat: 11-9, Sun 12-6

A nonprofit effort by the Mennonite Church, Ten Thousand Villages has branches around the country. It supports native artisans from around the world by promoting fair wages for handcrafters and fair prices for their work. It is an attractive store with interesting products for your home and lots of unusual gift ideas, like imported coffees, colorful textiles, mirrors, candles, cards, and holiday ornaments. I bought most of my holiday gifts here one year.

Kingsbury Chocolates

1017 King Street
Alexandria, VA 22314
703-548-2800
www.kingsburychocolates.com
Tues-Sat: 11-7

Opened in 2002 by Robert Kingsbury, this is heaven for a chocoholic. Handmade confections (truffles are a specialty), beverages, and pastries make this a great refueling stop, or a place to buy a little sweet treat for a loved one. Gift certificates are available. You can rationalize the calories because you have to climb a flight of stairs to get there.

J Brown & Co
1119 King Street
Alexandria, VA 22314
703-548-9010
Mon-Sat: 10-6, Sun: 12-6:

The gorgeous storefront—complete with awning, luxurious seasonal plantings, and antique bicycle—is enough to make you stop. Inside you'll find accessories for the home, like lamps, tchotchkes, soaps, candles, and napkin rings, that are, in a word, sumptuous. Everything just smells so good! The fabulous selection of silk flowers may be bought singly or in an innovative custom arrangement. This shop is OTT!

The Lamplighter
1207 King Street
Alexandria, VA 22314
703-549-4040
www.lamplighterlamps.com
Mon-Fri: 10-5:30, Sat: 10-5

This family-owned shop has been around forever, and it's where Alexandrians take their lamps for repair. It also has a large selection of new lamps and boasts the largest selection of lampshades in the area.

A Likely Story
1555 King Street
Alexandria, VA 22314
703-836-2498
www.alikelystorybooks.com
Mon-Sat: 10-6, Sun 1-5

Reading is an active endeavor at A Likely Story. Since 1984, this award-winning children's book store has fostered a love of reading—with everything from board books for babies to classics for young adults (both fiction and non-fiction) character puppets, music, and audio books. A monthly calendar lets you know about the story times that occur five days a week (Monday through Thursday and Saturday) at different hours to enable children of all ages to participate; there are writer's workshops, family nights, and book discussion groups. Add to that author visits and readings and frequent buyer discounts, and you have the perfect place to encourage your children to expand their world—and yours—through reading.

Alexandria-Del Ray

Del Ray was once a blue-collar neighborhood populated by railroad workers, but now it is a hot, and very different, community just north of Old Town. With a very active community organization and a real small-town feel, it is undergoing a vibrant revitalization with nearly overnight changes.

Del Ray Farmers' Market

Mt. Vernon Avenue and Oxford Street
Alexandria, VA 22301
www.radiodelray.com/drfm.html
Sat: 8-Noon (April-December)

If you get up late and miss the Old Town Market, the Del Ray Farmers' Market is a smaller, but excellent substitute. With stalls in a small parking lot, this market is primarily produce and flowers, but also includes gourmet mushrooms, exceptional artisan cheeses, and Best Buns bread.

Tops of Old Town, Inc.

2400 Mt. Vernon Avenue
Alexandria, VA 22301
703-836-4511
www.topsofoldtown.com
Mon-Fri: 10-6, Sat: 9-7, Sun: closed

Queen Elizabeth is missing out. She needs to hop across the pond and visit Tops of Old Town to get the best hats and matching suits (she doesn't need the jewelry because she has the crown jewels).

Willie Mae Mitchell has been providing fashion services and teaching the basics of "hattitude" in this modest corner location since 1991. If you start off with a "kindergarten" style, it really doesn't take too long to get your secondary diploma, but the graduate level—that's another story! Willie Mae and her daughter, Sheila, are warm, nurturing women, who are there to help you select just the right outfit (sizes 8 to 32) for any special occasion. Their customer service is unparalleled and forthright, believe me!

As for the hats, you really just have to see them for yourself. Swoops, swirls, sequins, rain hats, sun hats (everyone needs one!). I may just join the Red Hat Society and select one of Willie Mae's gorgeous options. There is quite a selection for men and children, as well. I bought myself a wide-brimmed, crushable, orange sun hat with a wonderful hat pin. Girls, I've got the hattitude!

Bonnie Greer & Company
2301 Mt. Vernon Avenue
Alexandria, VA 22301
703-683-4880
Wed-Fri: 11-7, Sat: 10-5:30; Sun: 12-5

With a very nice, although limited, assortment of well-made Adirondack and leather chairs, sofas, storage ottomans (the floor sample prices are quite tempting!), Hobo bags, Cat's Pajamas, bead jewelry, and interesting food items, Bonnie Greer is a friendly, interesting store that really invites a look around.

Eight Hands Round
116 East Del Ray Avenue
Alexandria, VA 22301
703-518-3058
Tues-Fri: 10-6, Sat: 9-5, Sun: 1-5

An eclectic mix of European folk art antiques, and lots of American-made items like Sara Schneidman cards and pillows, and beautiful handmade birdhouses, along with Nilia products, like lip balm, soap, and bath salts, that are handmade just up the street. There is a small, but exquisite, group of gifts for babies. Last time I visited, there was even an old red tricycle and a 1929 diet plan, complete with exercises, which are more relevant than you might think.

Remix
1906 Mt. Vernon Avenue
Alexandria, VA 22301
703-549-4110
Mon-Tues: 6-9 p.m., Wed-Fri: 11-9, Sat: 10-8, Sun: 12-5

Serious Funkadelic here. A plethora of polyester! Remix is the place to go for vintage clothing from the 60's and 70's. (I got the most fabulous tulle skirt for my 18-year-old niece—she is wild about it!) For some of us who actually wore this stuff in our youth, it might make us wonder what we were thinking, but I sort of wish those bright orange suits would come back in style. The prices are great and the shop looks care-free—just like we were.

Potomac West Interiors & Antique Gallery
1517 Mt. Vernon Avenue
Alexandria, VA 22314
703-519-1911
Tues-Sat: 10-6, Sun: 12-5

Five Oaks Antiques
2413 Mt. Vernon Avenue
Alexandria, VA 22301
703-519-7006
www.fiveoaksantiques.com
Tues-Sat: 10-6, Sun: 12-5

Susan Driscoll opened Potomac West in 1999, and followed with Five Oaks a few blocks away in 2002. Together, these two stores provide an excellent, eclectic antique experience. The idea is simple: rent space to individual dealers who stock your shops with an incredible variety of old, retro, sort-of-new, and a few new, hand-crafted items Both spaces are open, well-lit, and dust free; displays are tantalizing. And both locations have lower levels that are worth visiting. Potomac West has 15 to 17 dealers, and Five Oaks has over 30. Between the two of them, you will find little repetition, a wealth of nostalgia, and some interesting furniture and accessories that will make your house a home.

Eclectic Nature

1503 Mt. Vernon Avenue
Alexandria, VA 22301
703-837-0500
Tues-Fri 9-6, Sat 8-4, Sun 10-4

Just as she's been doing in gardens around Alexandria for years, Christy Beal has transformed an abandoned lot and unassuming bungalow into a colorful garden, art, and gift oasis. There's plenty of year-round appeal, with plants and garden accoutrements in the outdoor space (bet holiday greenery shows up in November!), and a wide-ranging selection of gifts, original art, and personal items inside. The strong colors and evocative painting, both inside and out are welcoming, and each room, including the bathroom, is a feast for the senses. Opened in mid-2004, this is a new venture, with a great location, and a bright future!

What's to Eat?

St. Elmo's Coffee Pub
2300 Mt. Vernon Avenue
703-739-9268 • www.stelmoscoffeepub.com
Early morning through the evening, Sunday till 6 pm only

For coffee and pastries go where the locals—go to the corner of Del Ray Avenue. Wednesday through Saturday evenings there's entertainment; visit their website for a schedule.

Del Ray Dreamery
2310 Mt. Vernon Avenue
703-683-7767 • www.delraydreamery.com
Mon-Sun: Seasonal

For real frozen custard and other tempting concoctions, try the Del Ray Dreamery. If you're lucky, you might stumble upon their once a month "brat" (bratwurst) night, when customers eat brats, drink ginger ale, and move to oompa music.

Mancini's Café
1508 Mt. Vernon Avenue
703-838-3663 • www.manciniscafe.com
Breakfast, lunch, dinner (no dinner on Sunday, Monday and Wednesday)

THE place for corned beef hash and home fries, along with tasty lunches and dinners.

Al's Steak House
1504 Mt. Vernon Avenue
703-836-9443 • www.alssteak.com
Lunch, dinner

And be sure not to miss Al's Steak House ("Alexandria's First and Foremost Philly Cheese Steak Shop") because "Uncle Al is our Nation's Pal!"

Alexandria-Hollin Hall

Alexandria, Fairfax County, the area just south of Alexandria's city limits (and the Beltway), has many subdivisions, like Belle Haven, the beautiful Mount Vernon Parkway with lots of trees, and the Route 1 corridor of strip malls. But, the Hollin Hall Shopping Center on Fort Hunt Road is like something you would find in a small town.

Hollin Hall Variety Store, Inc.
7902 Fort Hunt Road
Alexandria, VA 22308
703-765-4110
Mon-Sun: 9-9

Does anyone remember notions? Years ago, before retail specialization, all department stores—even Hecht's—had a notions department where you could buy zippers, buttons, thread, hooks and eyes, knitting needles, lingerie elastic, and other useful things to go with the sewing fabrics. When Charles (Ben) Vennell and his wife, Ann, established Hollin Hall Variety in October 1958, dress fabrics and patterns were a big part of the business. Today, it's quilting fabric, and, thankfully, the notions department is still in tact.

But this is a VARIETY store, and, boy, does it have variety. You can set up housekeeping—pots, pans, bath mats, shower curtains, curtain rods, detergent, paint, towels, you name it. Then you can give yourself a great housewarming party with invitations and decorations from their party supply department. Then, stop into the crafts department, where you can find what you need to create accessories to decorate your new home.

Holidays are a big thing here. It's a kid's dream for Halloween, and you just know Santa's elves are waiting in line, just behind the Thanksgiving Turkey, while the Easter Bunny waits in the wings. It's an extravaganza!

But the most wonderful thing about the Hollin Hall Variety Store is that it's still here after 45 years. In the year it opened, there were 193 variety stores in the Washington area. Today, there are three (see sidebar). That's because Mr. Vennell once refused an offer from the Ben Franklin chain, and he joined a co-op that works with variety store owners to enable them to buy at "big store" prices. So, not only can you find what you want, you can get it at a great price. It's a retail experience that Gap Kids have only dreamed of.

Two other variety stores in the area have distinct personalities, but the same type of great inventories. Both of them are worth the trip!

Ayers Variety and Hardware
Westover Shopping Center
5853 N. Washington Boulevard
Arlington, VA 22205
703-538-5678

Bruce's Variety Stores
6922 Arlington Road
Bethesda, MD 20814
301-656-7543

The Blossom Shop
7906 Fort Hunt Road
Alexandria, VA 22308
703-768-3410, 888-768-3410
703-768-3778 (fax)
Mon-Fri: 9:30-6, Sat: 9-5:30

This shop has more than flowers. Just stroll through the beautifully displayed gift items in this comfortable two-room store right next to the Hollin Hall Variety Store.

The Blossom Shop has been a fixture in this little strip of stores since 1967. Dorothy Trimber is its third owner, and she bought the shop a few years ago from the owners who were friends of the family. Dorothy is a young woman who always wanted her own business and loved flowers, so she jumped at the chance to continue a tradition. A member of Teleflora, she has flowers for all occasions, along with balloons and gourmet gift baskets. Her senior floral designer, Jean Clark, is well known in the community and has done quite a few of the area's weddings, funerals, and proms during her 25+ years in the business.

Among Dorothy's gift lines are Vera Bradley bags, Peggy Karr glassware, Thymes lotions and soaps, plus china, dolls, decorative accessories, and candles. It's a sweet smelling place to visit, and you'll probably not be able to leave empty handed.

What's to eat?

Hollin Hall Pastry Shop
7920 Fort Hunt Road
703-768-9643 • www.hollinhallpastry.com
Early morning through early evening, Sunday till 2 pm only

If you're thirsty and hungry after all this shopping, stroll on down to the Hollin Hall Pastry Shop for a nice cup of coffee and a tasty little pastry or cookie. They also have delicious and beautiful cakes to take home.

Arlington – Crystal City

In the 1960's, Charles E. Smith built Crystal City, the first mixed-use development in the Washington area. With condos, hotels, apartments, and offices above ground, he very wisely made the underground a meandering mall that has just about everything you might need to survive without ever having to go outside. There's even a Metro stop.

Ship's Hatch, Inc.

1677 Crystal Square Arcade
Arlington, VA 22202
703-413-6289
www.shipshatch.com
Mon-Fri: 10-7, Sat: 10-6

10376 Main Street
Fairfax, VA 22030
703-691-1670
Mon-Thurs: 10-6, Fri-Sat: 10-5

Mary Beth Cox and her husband started refinishing and building tables from salvaged ships' hatches back in 1973. Following a "fantastic" Washington Post story about their work, Mary Beth opened their first store in 1978 in Fairfax City. Then in 1984, Charles E. Smith made them an offer they couldn't refuse, and they added the Crystal City location.

The Ship's Hatch is a man's store, full of memories and memorabilia. Filled with one-of-a-kind nautical antiques, Mary Beth says the most common compliment is, "It's like walking through a museum." She buys her items from collectors and at antique shows, so if you see something you like, don't wait to buy it or you may be disappointed. She does search for special items on request, and sometimes hits the jackpot. Many of her customers are tourists or people who have heard about her unique selection and terrific sales staff—all of whom have military backgrounds.

Many old salts proudly wear embroidered ships caps created by the Ship's Hatch. That's because the store owns the silhouettes of the 16,000 ships in American military history, from the USS Constitution to the latest aircraft carrier, and can produce special caps in any quantity, starting at one. You can see a selection of the caps on their website, but a visit to either of their stores is much better. They have also added merchandise that is appropriate for all of the services, so if ships aren't your bag, they will surely have an airplane or something else to suit.

The first 3,000 ship's hatch tables were sold long ago, and many other wonderful things have taken their place. But, as fate would have it, another limited number of hatches have been found and the Ship's Hatch is once again creating the tables that started it all.

The Men's Shop Ltd.
2156 Crystal Plaza Arcade
Arlington, VA 22202
703-415-0330
Mon-Sat: 10-6

Don't forget the men in your life. Since 1967, proprietor Joe Kanawati has maintained a variety of suits, sport coats, sweaters, and gorgeous ties. There's something soothing about this little one-room shop with its personal service and small assortment of select merchandise. It's the type of men's store that our grandfathers may have frequented, and that still attracts a discriminating type of man.

Crystal Boutique
2160 Crystal Plaza Arcade
Arlington, VA 22202
703-415-1400, 800-413-1404
www.crystalboutique.com
Mon-Sat: 10-6 (Tues & Thurs until 8)

Hidden away in the Crystal City Underground since 1971 is an elegant boutique that prides itself on making fashion accessible. Joel Cohen, whose mother opened the store all those years ago, now runs the bright, comfortable space with his wife, Amy. They take great pleasure in their personalized service and the close relationships they've developed with their customers. My friend Patti travels all the way from Southern Maryland to shop at the boutique.

The clothing selection ranges from casual to career, from the latest styles and fabrics to classic cuts and traditional blends. In addition to a wide range of designer labels, they carry a line of custom knits, similar to St. John, that are cut to fit in your choice of color and styles. Shearling coats are a specialty, as well. Joel and his staff help women discover clothing styles and colors that they never knew they could wear and enjoy. It is not a one-size-fits-all experience, because fit is an important part of the mix. They carry sizes up to 3X and will alter or special-order items to meet your specifications.

During a recent visit, a lovely shopper told me that she has shopped at the Crystal Boutique for many years because they take the intimidation factor out of buying fine clothes that last a lifetime. And that's something.

Arlington— Lee Heights Shops

There they sit, all in a row, just off Lee Highway at Lorcom Lane and Old Dominion Boulevard, waiting to be discovered—if you haven't discovered them already! It's a well-rounded shopping area filled with small business owners with big ideas: food, wine, decoration (personal and home), books, toys, beauty. Whadayaneedamallfor?

Pastries by Randolph
4500 Lee Highway
Arlington, VA 22207
703-243-0700
Mon-Fri: 6:30-6:30, Sat: 8-5, Sun: 8-1

Pastries, cookies, butter cream cakes, wedding cakes, special occasion cakes—they are all great. Call and they'll send you a wedding cake brochure.

Arrowine

4508 Lee Highway
Arlington, VA 22207
703-525-0990
www.arrowine.com
Mon-Sat: 10-8; Sun: 10-4

Need some cheese to go with that wine? There's a great selection here—and they give you a nibble before you buy. Discounts on wine are 10% on one case (full or mixed), 15% on three cases, 20% on four or more cases. They also carry fresh H&H Bagels (New York's best), a large selection of olives, and other appropriate nibbles.

Kinder Haus Toys

4510 Lee Highway
Arlington, VA 22207
703-527-5929
www.kinderhaus.com
Mon-Fri: 10-7, Sat: 10-6, Sun: 10-4

Kinder Haus has two floors of specialty toys and attractions, like the dungeon installed for Halloween. It's wide selection includes wooden toys, children's craft and hobby supplies, darling clothing, and Madame Alexander dolls. The store provides complementary gift wrap, newsletters, an on-line catalog, and special events. It's the sister store to Imagination Station—just down the row.

Prince Street
4514 Lee Highway
Arlington, VA 22207
703-524-1048
Mon-Fri: 10-6, Sat: 10-5:30, Sun: 12-4

Feast your eyes on an exceptional selection of elegant and fun gifts, books, cards, candles, calendars, cookbooks, serving utensils and platters, occasional tables and mirrors, paper goods, frames, tableware, and a little bit of everything. Now I know where my friend Beverlee gets all those great gifts for me! If you can't find something for every person you have ever known, look harder, because I bet it's there. Owner Sally Prince also owns Lemon Chiffon & Lemon Twist right next door. Prince Street has a gift registry and free gift wrapping—what more can you ask for?

Lemon Chiffon & Lemon Twist
4518 Lee Highway
Arlington, VA 22207
703-524-4680
Mon-Fri: 10-6, Sat: 10-5:30, Sun: 11-4

A specialty boutique for women, with a small selection of ties for men, this store doesn't have anything that the department stores have. Sizes 2 through 16, a few shoes, accessories, Vera Bradley bags, with emphasis on elegant and everyday casual—it's a great place to browse or buy: your choice.

Pamela Wright Interiors

4522 Lee Highway
Arlington, VA 22207
703-243-5600
Mon-Sat: 10-5:30

Sick of the way your house looks? Do it over from top to bottom with new rugs, draperies, furniture, wall color, fabrics, and accessories. It's available all in one place with expert guidance.

Imagination Station

4524 Lee Highway
Arlington, VA 22207
703-522-2047
www.kinderhaus.com/imagine
Mon-Fri: 10-7, Sat: 10-6, Sun: 10-4

Wish this store had been around when I was a kid. This children's bookstore has 25,000 titles in stock (a few are for grownups). Some are in foreign languages, some are on tape. Every Friday there's a story hour and you may meet a favorite character or author when you least expect it. Teachers and librarians get professional discounts, and there's a frequent buyer card that really works. It's the sister store to Kinder Haus Toys up the row.

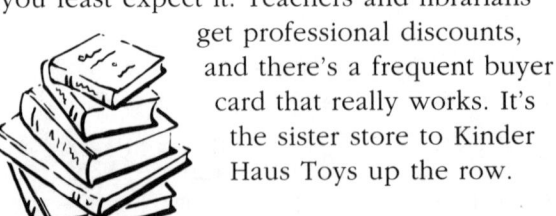

Lee Heights Florist
4528 Lee Highway
Arlington, VA 22207
703-522-4002, 877-562-4002
703-522-4048 (fax)
www.leeheightsflorist.net
Mon-Fri: 10-6, Sat: 10-5, Sun: 12:15-4

Family-owned and serving Falls Church, Arlington, and McLean, you can place orders on-line 24 hours a day. You can also walk in and buy some posies to brighten your day or someone else's. What could be better?

Facets
4530 Lee Highway
Arlington, VA 22207
703-527-4247
Tues-Fri: 10-5:30, Sat: 10-5, Sun: 12-3

Jewels—every body needs embellishment. Facets owners, Tom and Suzanne Arnold, specialize in custom design, and work with customers to create their visions. They also do in-house repairs, and carry a wide selection of fine jewelry, some estate pieces, and an interesting mix of contemporary and classic silver jewelry.

*Also in Arlington, see **Ayers Variety and Hardware** (Alexandria—Hollin Hall).*

WHAT'S TO EAT?

Café Parisien Express
4520 Lee Highway
703-525-3332
Breakfast, lunch, dinner, Sunday brunch

A Washingtonian magazine Best Bargain Restaurant, Café Parisien Express feels a little like St. Germain de Pres. Family owned by a French wife (chef) and Greek husband (manager), it features authentic French food, at great prices, and a full catering menu.

Cassatt's Café
4536 Lee Highway
703-894-0504 • www.cassatts.com
Breakfast, lunch, dinner (no dinner on Sunday)

This is a great place for an artful nosh. Tasty soups, salads, sandwiches, and an art school in the basement operated by the Arlington Artists Alliance. Artworks on the wall are for sale, and at Family Night, every Thursday evening from 6-8, parents come for dinner, while their children have an art attack!

Pollo a la Brasa
4540 Lee Highway
703-243-4222
Lunch, dinner

After a hard day of shopping, carry home some mouth-watering rotisserie chicken with all the trimmings. Prepared the South American way, it's some of the best chicken in the area, and they have awards to prove it. The side dishes are very special, too, especially the yams!

McLean

What was once farmland has turned into urban sprawl, but upscale sprawl. No trailer parks here. But there is some pretty interesting shopping to be had. Here are a few great spots to start with.

Mae's Dress Boutique
6707 Old Dominion Drive
McLean, VA 22101
703-356-6333
www.maesdress.com
Mon-Sat: 10-5:30

So, you've been invited to a charity ball/cocktail party/Bar Mitzvah/the White House. And, of course, you have nothing to wear. Well, just head on over to Mae's Dress Boutique. If you can't find something there, you might as well decline the invitation!

My very fashionable neighbor Nancy introduced me to Mae's. She told me I had no idea, and I hadn't! From the outside, the shop is unassuming, and once inside, it's not really fancy. No frills, just racks and racks of gorgeous gowns, mother-of-the-bride dresses, chic suits, flowing afternoon dresses, cocktail dresses, classic casuals, sportswear, and even a little leather.

Mae Shipe says she had big dreams and after 28 years, she says, "They all came true!" With hundreds of brands, she has the area's premier selection of "After 5" attire in sizes 4 to 24. And because she handpicks everything in stock, and doesn't buy by the gross, you don't stand much chance of passing yourself on the street or on the dance floor. Mae's has couture lines, and can do special orders depending on the supplier. Although she travels to New York to buy most of her stock, top designers from around the country come to her with their best designs. Please note: they do not carry bridal or bridesmaids' dresses.

The sales staff mirrors Mae's attention to detail. Nearly all of her employees have been with her for 20-plus years and know the stock. I doubt if anyone who is looking for something special goes away empty handed, because these ladies have the ability to zero in on exactly what you need! So, if you are looking for something classic, sophisticated, and timeless, a stop at Mae's Dress Boutique is what's needed.

The Artisans
Langley Shopping Center
1368 Chain Bridge Road
McLean, VA 22101
703-506-0158
www.artisansofmclean.com
Hours: Mon-Fri: 10-6 (Thurs until 7)

Thank you, Knowles, for sending me to Artisans! Owners Judith Leary Harkins and Shannon Denny Price began small at the Evans Farm Co-op in 1984 and just got bigger and bigger, but not too big. In fact, Artisans is just right.

Judith says it's a shop with 10,000 earrings—most made by local artists—but there are also lots of other creative things to fill up the rest of the space and to covet, from clothing to tchochkees to handmade gift items. While they do carry brands that are well-known in the arts and crafts community, like Hillborn Pottery, Ayala Bar jewelry, Maralyce Farrar coats, Artisans loves to stock local items. Among them are beautiful wooden boxes made by John Mendes. And they are looking for other local potters, clothing designers, or woodworkers to add to their inventory.

Like many other small enterprises, this is a shop with a social conscience. Judith and Shannon sponsor activities for charities, like gift wrapping services at the holidays to benefit Child Help, periodic benefits for groups, such as Martha's Table and Suited for Change. Artisans is a place that is definitely worth a visit, a browse, or a buy.

*Also in McLean, see District of Columbia listing for **Tree Top Toys** (Foxhall Square).*

WHAT'S TO EAT?

Three Pigs Barbecue
1394 Chain Bridge Road
703-356-1700
Lunch, dinner

This unassuming place reminds me of the old Dixie Pig Barbecues, with a similar menu. It is in the same strip as Artisans, so just park and walk.

Falls Church

Did you know that the community of Falls Church is over 300 years old? Established as the intersection of two Indian trails (now Leesburg Pike and Lee Highway), early settlers built the first permanent structure in 1699. The settlement expanded from there with the construction of the Alexandria-Leesburg turnpike in 1840 and the arrival of the railroad in 1859. Today, Falls Church is an independent, "All American" city, with lively shopping and many amenities—here are just a few.

Foxes Music

416 S. Washington Street
Falls Church, VA 22046
703-533-7393, 800-446-4414
www.foxesmusic.com
Mon-Thurs: 10-8, Fri-Sat: 10-6, Sun: 12-5

I certainly don't know who needs the complete songbook of Ozzy Osbourne (unless it's Ozzy), but my friend Elizabeth, who plays several instruments, really likes Foxes. Since 1953, it's been in the business of supplying everything for the musician, student, and teacher. In the words of a long-time employee, it's "inventory laden."

You'll find printed music—all styles, periods, flavors—the choral and piano departments are the largest; instruments for bands and orchestras (sales or rentals for the school market), video sales and rentals of great performances and instruction in things like jazz guitar.

If you can't play an instrument, you can get lessons in the store or privately, and they do repair instruments (but don't guarantee you perfect pitch). For those hard-to-buy-for musician friends, you can find a gift that's right on key or give a gift certificate. The best part is that many of the sales staff have been around for 20 years or more, so please ask for help or suggestions.

They do a great mail order business, but you can't order on their website, so like the sign says, "If practice gets you to Carnegie Hall, then Foxes Music in Falls Church is a great place to stop along the way."

Upscale Resale Quality Consignments
8100 Lee Highway
Falls Church, VA 22042
703-698-8100
www.upscale-resale.com
Mon-Fri: 10-7, Sat: 12-6, Sun: 12-5

Upscale Resale defies description. You think you have it pinned down, and poof! The image disappears. That's because you never know what you'll discover. Chairs, dressers, sofas, end tables, antiques, mirrors, accessories, rugs, lamps…the inventory is transitory. Founded in 1992 by Bob and Lib Willey, Upscale Resale is a true family business and a stroke of genius. The 28,000 square-foot store (the largest in the metro area) is a maze of rooms packed with plenty of things to attract your attention.

Everything in the store is there on individual or manufacturer consignment. Items can be perfect or not, and all are sold "as is." Prices start at reasonable and then drop every seven days for a month until the price is low, low, low. (Their slogan is "Prices drop until you shop.") Buying at Upscale Resale is a little like playing poker: you've got to know when to hold 'em... . If you know you can't live without that two-piece, French inlaid armoire in perfect condition, pay the starting price ($900) or hold on for a month and pay a third of that.

On my last visit, there were Tibetan chests, a church pew, some great wicker furniture, and some ornate marble-top sideboards. If you get what you want, but can't get it home, Gulliver's Movers has a freight desk where you can arrange delivery. If you just feel

"Upscale Resale is a true family business and a stroke of genius."

the need to start over and sell everything you own, there are rules for consigning available at the front door. If you're into self-service, calculated risk, and bargain prices, Upscale Resale is definitely a friendly, fair, and fun place to shop.

Fairfax Glass Company
7728 Lee Highway
Falls Church, VA 22042
703-560-1140
Hours: Mon-Fri: 8:30-5 (Thurs until 6),
  Sat 9:30-12:30

If you go a little further east on Lee Highway, you'll come to Fairfax Glass Company. If you need a good mirror at a reasonable price, this is where you'll find it. Fairfax Glass is really a construction glass company that does large commercial jobs, but they've converted the front of their shop into a showroom that is filled with a huge selection of top quality, beautifully framed mirrors. With a wide variety of sizes and styles that will fit anywhere and match any décor, these are quality mirrors that will last for generations. I'm not sure they have any magic mirrors in stock, but you can ask.

Woodburners Two
6600 Arlington Boulevard
Falls Church, VA 22042
703-241-1400
www.woodburnerstwo.com
Mon-Fri: 10-6 (Thurs until 8), Sat: 10-5

What's better or more romantic than a fireplace on a cold winter's day? Woodburners Two is the place to go to fulfill your fireplace fantasy. From the White House to the embassies to your very own home, an elegant fireplace with all the accessories is their specialty. Oh, you don't have a chimney? They can install one! How about a beautiful mantel and inviting hearth? They can do that, too! Gas logs? Inserts for both old and new construction? Come on in! A fireplace from Woodburners Two is a turnkey operation.

Margaret Laurenson and Judy Miller (the two in the store name) identified a need 25 or so years ago and have built an extensive selection, along with a loyal and satisfied clientele. They work with folks who are interested in improving their existing fireplace, creating a fireplace in new construction, or just adding a fireplace anywhere in their home. They even have "fakes" a la 1950 with electric flames to simulate that burning feeling. They also have fireplace doors, beautiful fire screens, andirons, and tools. My husband is a real wood guy, but even he was impressed by the Paul Bunyan gas logs made by Golden Blount. (You can even get the crackle with battery-operated pine cones that play wood fire sounds.) They also carry Vermont Castings and Heatilator brands.

But this is a year-round operation, so they've thoughtfully included garden accessories, benches, birdhouses, mailboxes, and awnings in their inventory. The perfect place for a "house-warming" gift, don't you think?

Vienna

Just past Tyson's Corner, there is Maple Avenue, the heart of Vienna, and a far cry from the malls. Church Street runs parallel to Maple and has several attractions that are worth a detour.

Star's Beads, Ltd.
139 A Church Street, NW
Vienna, VA 22180
703-938-7018
www.starsbeads.com
Mon-Fri: 10-6, Sat: 10-5, Sun: 12-4

Several years ago, I met a lovely woman named Beverlee who always wore fabulous jewelry. I asked where she got it, and when she said she made it and would teach me how, I was hooked! The first place she took me was Star's Beads. What a find!

After spending two years as a "traveling bead store" while teaching full time, Star McGivern moved her burgeoning business out of her home, ended her 20-year teaching career, and opened the shop in 1996—at the height of a snowstorm and the bottom of the bead market. Now, beads are hotter than ever, and with her extensive inventory and excellent prices, Star's Beads is a must-shop for Bead Queens and wanna bees.

"...a must-shop for Bead Queens and wanna bees"

In this small, off-the-beaten-path location, Star has an international bead inventory: her buying trips take her to Bangkok, Mexico, Russia, Tunisia, Italy, Morocco—just about anywhere there are beads to be had. Because she does her own buying without the help of a middleman, all of her beads are fairly priced, as her loyal clientele will attest. She has antique beads, tribal beads, semi-precious beads, glass, crystals, stone, polymer, plastic—the list goes on. And then there are all the findings needed to create the finished product. Ever mindful of the necessary niche, Star has collected over 150 styles of clasps that are available in the shop and on her website.

If you don't have a clue as to what to do with all of these choices, Star's Beads has developed an extensive class schedule that features great instructors who teach a wide variety of skills from pearl knotting to table-top soldering and wire wrapping, and show you how to create projects. It's possible to spend as little as two hours and go home with a finished piece that will stun and amaze your family and friends. But, be careful—it's addictive.

Consignment Boutique

141-A Church Street, NW
Vienna VA. 22180
703-281-0759
Mon-Fri: 10-6, Sat: 10-5

Secondhand stores can be like rusty used cars, but this one is sort of like a pre-owned Lexus. It's bright, neat, and well-stocked, and the displays are attractive. The consignment term is only two months, so the stock changes constantly. They also have quite a collection of tableware, lamps, and gift items—many of them never used.

The Brambled Nest
141 Church Street, NW
Vienna VA 22180
703-319-3277
Mon-Sat: 10-6 (Thurs until 7), Sun: 12-5

With its display of old and new outdoor/garden furniture, pots, and decorations right outside the door, the Brambled Nest is enticing. After you finish with the wonderful outside, the inside is filled with a wide variety of "stuff": stuff to give away, stuff to keep, stuff that makes you laugh, stuff you need, stuff you can't resist.

The Artful Gift Shop
145 B Church Street, NW
Vienna, VA 22180
703-242-1220
Weds-Sat: 10-6, Sun: 1-5

If you are looking for a handcrafted gift made by local artisans at a reasonable price, Kim Silhanek has quite the collection of earrings, frames, mirrors, and decorative items. It's a small area, painted the most glorious color, that testifies to the great creativeness of our area craftspeople.

Earth and Fire
144 Church Street, NW
Vienna, VA 22180
703-255-3107
www.earthandfiregallery.com
Tues-Sun: 10-5, Sun: 1-5

Here's an innovative way to stock your shop: give artisans a dollar amount and they ship what they want. So, every shipment is a surprise, and the collection of functional and art pottery, wood items, and glassware is quite diverse and creative. Be sure to check out the one-of-a-kind Bula Bags.

What's to eat?

Nielsen's Frozen Custard
144 Church Street, NW
703-255-5553
Late morning through the evening

Right across the street is Nielsen's Frozen Custard. My friend KTJ has a love affair with the amalgamation called Concrete. Unfortunately (or not), she lives in Geneva, Switzerland, but the next time she "comes across the pond," one of our first stops will be at Nielsen's for a tasty grinder and a cup of real frozen custard in Chocolate or Vanilla with a little something special mixed in.

Springfield

Don't be afraid of Springfield. It's been looking bad lately because of all of the I-95 construction. And speaking of construction, when I need to do a little around the house, I venture out that way to my favorite hardware store in the world.

Fischer's Hardware
6129 Backlick Road
Springfield, VA 22041
703-451-3700
Mon-Fri: 9-9, Sat: 9-6, Sun: 1-4

My friend Karen is a very handy woman. She loves Fischer's Hardware because she can find that elusive hardware she needs to maintain her older home. I love Fischer's because I just plain love hardware stores. The first time I visited Fischer's, I was dumbstruck—

"I felt my credit card move."

just stood there in the middle of the aisle overwhelmed by the sheer volume of stuff arranged neatly and categorically. I felt my credit card move. If you want an O-ring, they have every size. Need a hammer? Bird feeder? Flower pot? Snow shovel? Paint? Automotive supplies? They have just about whatever you want.

Now, you can get these things at Home Depot or Lowe's, but at Fischer's, you actually have someone who knows where things are and will help you find them! In fact, gentlemen in black vests roam the store asking shoppers, "Are you finding everything you need?" It's revolutionary! Customer service! You pay a little more for the effort, but if you want a real old-time experience—they've been doing it for over four decades—it's worth the trip to Springfield. Don't let the ever-changing Springfield interchange construction deter you; call first and a nice person will give you excellent directions.

Occoquan

WORTH THE TRIP—*This little historic village in Prince William County is nestled on the Occoquan River right off I-95. It was settled in 1736 and was an active community with cotton mills, ship building, and the first ice storage house in the area. In the 20th century, it was devastated by fire, and hurricanes, but many of the historic buildings survive (some with ghosts). It's now a shopping destination or a place to decompress on the way back to Washington after a trip to Potomac Mills. There are lots of little places to browse, but here are a few great ones.*

Hawthorne House

404 Mill Street
Occoquan, VA 22125
703-491-5775
703-494-0084 (fax)
www.hawthornehouse.cceasy.com
Tues-Sat: 10:30-5, Sun: 12-5

There are special times in life when there is no substitute for a special printed announcement, invitation, or acknowledgement. Diane and Fred Boli knew this, so they opened Hawthorne House in 1984 to provide beautiful ways to communicate those special times.

When people think of invitations, they think of weddings. This little shop in a little house on Mill Street has an entire room devoted to wedding invitations and stationery. Did you know you can get scratch-off Save the Date cards? They also stock tons of other clever, colorful, contemporary, and classic invitations for the showers, the bridesmaids luncheons, and every other festivity surrounding that big event.

Think of all the other reasons to celebrate and communicate out there—births, birthdays, anniversaries, graduations, holidays, ceremonies, sporting events, reunions, dinners, lunches. No matter what anyone says, a written or printed invitation means a whole lot more than an e-mail one. Hawthorne House recognizes that, so they have everything you need to make whatever kind of celebration you have in mind a success, including printed napkins, glassware, and those favors every one is favoring.

There's also a well-organized website, where you can view many of their invitation choices, request samples, and even order online. But, a visit is the best way to see their selection, because then you can check out their gift line. While you're there, order yourself some personal stationery. It makes all of your correspondence special.

Details by Ursula
206 Mill Street
Occoquan, VA 22125
703-494-4959
Mon-Fri: 10-5, Sat: 10-6, Sun: 12-5

I'm not sure if it is the bright display of clothing hanging on the front porch or Ursula herself that makes Details so appealing. This little shop in the middle of historic Occoquan is a retail toddler—just a few years old—but it has lots of grown-up clothing and accessories. Owner Ursula Lafond describes her clients as "fabulous, real women." Her selection ranges from XS to XL (and larger) and features designers that specialize in comfortable casual clothing, such as Two Star Dog, Russ Behrens, Flax, Click, and Willow, and many lines that are American-made.

Shopping at Details is a lot like shopping with a girlfriend. Ursula will give you an honest opinion about whatever you try on. (After all, her slogan is "if you don't look good, we don't look good.") She always has terrific sale racks, and doesn't play around with small discounts. Her "oddballs" rack has some real bargains. At the end of the season, everything must go: she starts her sales at half-price, and what doesn't sell is donated to women's shelters.

Details also has a limited, but fun, collection of greeting cards, magnets, socks, and gift items for you and your friends. But, if you're in Occoquan, drop into Ursula's and get the Details for yourself!

Brambles
307 Mill Street
Occoquan, VA 22125
703-492-0401
www.occoquan.com
Hours: Mon-Fri: 10-5, Sun: 12-5

While you're wandering around, stop by Brambles for an eclectic mix of furnishings, (including a comfy line of slipcovered furniture from Lee) garden-themed gifts and accessories, and interesting hand painted furniture.

What's to Eat?

The Virginia Grill
Occoquan Inn
301 Mill Street • www.occoquaninn.com
Breakfast, lunch, dinner

For a bite to eat, in colonial-like surroundings, the Virginia Grill fits the bill with its menus of sandwiches, soups, and platters.

Purcellville

WORTH THE TRIP—*When it was founded in the late 18th century, the settlement was known as Purcel's Store (isn't that appropriate?). Before the Civil War, it became Purcellville, and troops marched through the area on their way to nearby battles. You might notice that all the buildings are stone, brick, or concrete. That's because a series of fires destroyed the town in the early 20th century and the town fathers decreed that wood buildings were not acceptable. But, wood furniture is allowed.*

Samuel S. Case

120 West Main Street
Purcellville, VA 20134
540-338-2725
Mon-Sat: 10-5, Sun: 12-5

My college roommate Barbara is a smart and a frugal woman. When she recommended that I check out Samuel S. Case furniture, I knew it would be worth the trip. So, one sunny day, my friend Karen and I hopped in the car and drove the 60 miles to Purcellville.

I'd seen the advertisements for Samuel S. Case many times, and was always intrigued. Barbara, who lives in Harper's Ferry, saw one in her local paper for "a terrific Columbus Day sale," and went in search of a sofa. Keep in mind that she had looked "up and down Rockville Pike, in Baltimore, Hagerstown, all the usual 'interior' stores which were either closed or the merchandise was ho-hum." When she finally got to Case, she was in heaven. Not only did it have spacious showrooms and good prices, but it was also on "a small town main street that had a corner luncheonette." Very Barbara.

And as it turned out, it was very Karen, as well! The salesperson was mature and definitely not pushy. She knew the answers to all our questions and provided helpful suggestions. We learned that Samuel S. Case is a real person who started in the antique business in 1989. When he kept getting requests for dining room tables, and the supply dwindled to nothing, he started making them himself. The beginning of a good thing, it seems.

Today, the antiques are gone, but what remains has the potential for "antiquehood." He has fine hardwood tables and chairs—many of them period reproductions—along with upholstered pieces from Southwood and a private label manufacturer. While most everything is custom-made, you can get some serious deals when a sale comes around, or when something hasn't sold. (There was an elegant dining room set with eight upholstered chairs that was priced almost at cost.) There are also many tasteful decorative items scattered throughout the showroom, which is NOTHING like Mastercraft or any of the big furniture stores.

When we left, Karen had bought a gorgeous, tomato red, microfiber sofa that was reduced by 50 percent. It's so comfortable I'm going back to see if I can find a similar deal.

What's to eat?

Candelora's
Purcellville Inn
36855 W. Main Street
540-338-2075
Lunch and dinner, Friday-Sunday Brunch (closed Mondays)

If you need to eat and corner luncheonettes aren't your speed, drive up the road to Candelora's at the Purcellville Inn. We had a casual lunch in the pub downstairs, but the upstairs—with its white tablecloths, fireplaces, and an Italian menu—warrants a return tasting trip.

Index

7-way Wonder Dress, 17
7th Street, SE, 2
8th Street, SE, 3-9
14th Street, NW, 10-14
18th Street, NW, 32
20th Street, NW, 28
34th Street, 71, 74
44th Street, NW, 40

A Likely Story, 95
A. Litteri, Inc., 5
A Little Shop of Flowers, 31
A Mano, 22
Abrielle, 35
action figures, 65
Adams Mill Road, NW, 30, 31
Adams Morgan, 30-32, 58
afghans, 92
African items, *see* Afrocentric items
Afrocentric items, 16, 74-75
Agapanthus, 31
Alexandria, 86-105,
Alexandria City Hall, 86
Alexandria Farmers' Market, The, 86
Alexis David, 8
All About Jane, 32
Al's Steak House, 101
Alvear Studio, 8
American Crafts Council, 56
American Flyer, 65
American Society of Appraisers, 27
Andrea Lieu, 44

antique books, 26-27
antique prints, 27
antiques, 2, 4, 39, 42, 65, 98, 99, 106, 119
aquariums, 63-65
Arlington, 32, 105-114
Arlington Boulevard, 121
Arlington Road, 103
Arnold, Tom and Suzanne, 113
aromatherapy, 51
Arrowine, 110
art, 2, 8, 10-11, 16, 39, 42, 51, 68, 88-89, 92-93, 100
Art and Soul, 5
Art League of Alexandria, The, 89
art supplies, 89
Artful Gift Shop, The, 125
Arthur M. Sackler Gallery of Art, The, 45
Artisan Lamp Company, 39
Artisans, The, 116
arts and crafts, 2, 5, 51, 56-57, 87, 88-89, 91-92, 92-93, 117, 125, 126
arts, performing, 2
Ashford, Snowden, 3
Asian items, 45
awnings, 122
Ayala Bar, 117
Ayers Variety and Hardware, 103, 113

Backlick Road, 127
Backstage, Inc., 7

bags, 9, 15, 20, 23, 37, 40, 74, 97, 104, 111, 126
baked goods, 2, 51, 66, 76, 87, 93, 96, 109
bakery, 76
baking supplies, *see* cake baking and decorating supplies
balloons, 104
balsamic vinegar, 6
Baltimore Avenue, 70
Banana Café and Piano Bar, 9
Barbarian, 61
Barracks Row, 6-9
Barry's Magic Shop, Ltd., 58
bath salts, 98
bathing suits, 54
beads, 123-124
Beal, Christy, 100
Beamo, 34
beards, 8
Bedhead, 9
bedsheets, 35
bellbottoms, 69
belts, *see* accessories
Ben Nye makeup, 8
benches, 122
Ben's Chili Bowl, 13
Berkeley Springs, W.V., 24, 25
Bethesda, 20, 26, 30, 50-58
Bethesda Avenue, 20, 26
bibles, 61
birdhouses, 98, 122
Bittenger, Margie, 62
Black Earth, 75
Blossom Shop, The, 104
Blue Arrowana, 64
Blue Moon, 43

Blue Willi, 36
bondage bed, 21
Bonifant Books, 60
Bonnie Greer & Company, 97
books, 14, 26-27, 34, 45, 46, 47, 59, 60, 61, 67, 75, 88, 91, 109, 111
books, children, 33-34, 89, 95, 112
Brambled Nest, The, 125
Brambles, 131
bras, fittings after breast surgery, 54
breads, *see* baked goods
breast prosthesis, 54
brewpub, 70
bridal gowns, 68
bridal registries, 22, 54
bridesmaids' dresses, 28
Brown, Warren, 18
Bruce's Variety Stores, 58, 103
B.T. McElrath, 43
Bula Bags, 126
Burg, Debbie, 42
Bush, Barbara, 41

Caddie, 41
Café Parisien Express, 114
cafes, *see* restaurants
cake baking and decorating supplies, 62-63
cake decorating class, 63
Cakelove, 18
cakes, 77
calendars, 14, 43
California products, 56
Cameron Street, 90, 91
Canadian products, 56
Canal Square, 24
candelabras, 61

Candelora's, 134
candied violets, 90
candles, 14, 15, 37, 43, 70, 93, 94, 104, 111
candy, 43
candy making, 62-63
canine treats, 51
Capitol Hill, 2-6, 14
caps, 106
Carol's Daughter, 74
Carroll Avenue, 66-68, 69
Carter, Rosalyn, 41
Casabella, 54
Cassett's Café, 114
cat suit, 21
Catch Can, 44
catering, 77
Catoctin Mountains, 77
Cat's Pajamas,
CDs, 27
ceramics, *see* pottery
Chain Bridge Road, 33, 116, 117
chairs, 5, 97, 119, 133
Chantal, 54
cheese, 6, 96, 110
Chellgren, Sarah, 9
Chevy Chase, 50, 53-54
Child Help, 117
China, 104
chocolates, 43, 93
Christmas ornaments, *see* holiday ornaments
Christopher Williams, 28
Church Street, 123-126
Clarendon Boulevard, 32
Clark, Jean, 104
Cleveland Park, 37-39,

Cleveland, President Grover, 37
Click, 130
clothing, children, 33, 36, 38, 44, 87, 89, 92, 110
clothing, men, 107
clothing, women, 2, 4, 5, 9, 15, 17, 20, 21, 28, 30, 32, 35-36, 36, 38, 44, 45, 68-69, 87, 91, 97, 98, 108, 111, 115, 117, 130
Cluss, Adolph, 3
coffees, 93
Cohen, Joel and Amy, 108
comics, 61
confections, 93
Connecticut Avenue, NW, 24, 38, 39, 42, 44
Consignment Boutique, 124
cookbooks, 91
co-ops, 71-73
cooperatives, 71-73
costumes, 7-8
Cox, Mary Beth, 106
crafts, *see* arts and crafts
Crane, 25
crystal, 22, 42
Crystal Boutique, 108
Crystal City, 105-109
Crystal Plaza Arcade, 107, 108
Crystal Square Arcade, 106
Cunningham Falls State Park, 77
Cut-Loose, 44

Daisy, 30, 58
Daisy Too, 30
Daly, Scott, 81
dancewear, 8
Dansko, 44

Dashikis, 74
Davidsonville, 80
Dean and DeLuca, 43
decorative accessories, *see* housewares
decorative arts, 16
Dekelbaum, 66
Del Ray, 95-101
Del Ray Avenue, 98
Del Ray Dreamery, 101
Del Ray Farmers' Market, 96
delicatessen, 2, 5, 66
Democracy Boulevard, 55
Desserts by Gerard, 76
Details by Ursula, 130
dialect tapes, 7
Discount Fabrics, 78
District of Columbia,
dolls, 75, 104, 110
Donna Baptiste, 28
Doyle, Chris, 72
draperies, 112
Dream Dresser, 21
dressers, 119
Driscoll, Susan, 99
drums, 67, 75
Dupont Circle, 24-29, 58
DVDs, 59

earrings, 5, 117, 125
Earth and Fire, 126
Eastern Market, 2-4, 6, 11
eateries, *see* restaurants
Eclectic Nature, 100
eggs, 3, 51
Eight Hands Round, 98
Eighth Street, SE,

Elder Crafters of Alexandria, Inc., 91
Ella Moss, 30
Elm Street, 51, 52
English items, 22
Evans Farm Co-op, 116
evening wear, 68
eyeglass cases, 40
eyeglasses, 17, 44, 51, 68

fabric, 78-79, 112
Facets, 113
Fairfax Glass Company, 121
Falls Church, 118-122
farmers' markets, 2, 86, 96
feather boas, 8
fiber arts, 88
Finewares, 68
Finials, 42
Firehook Bakery, 73
Fireplace tools, 122
fireplaces, 121
Fischer's Hardware, 127
fish, 64, 82
Five Oaks Antiques, 99
Flanagan, Jackie, 15
Flax, 44, 130
flea market, 2, 4, 51
flowers, 2, 13, 31, 50, 87, 96, 104, 113
fog machines, 82
folk instruments, *see* musical instruments
food, 2, 3, 4, 5, 50, 70, 71-73, 71-73, 87, 96, 97, 109, 110
food co-op, 71-73
food, dogs, 51

Fort Hunt Road, 102-105
fountains, 82
Foxes Music, 118
Foxhall Square, 33-37
frames, 43, 111, 125
Franklin's, 70
Free People, 30
Freer Gallery of Art, 45
French products, 22, 35, 54
Friendship Heights, 39-44
F Street, NW, 46
furniture, 5, 8, 16, 21, 39, 40, 42, 44, 45, 55-56, 81, 97, 99, 112, 119-120, 125, 131, 133
furniture designer, 17

gadgets, 38, 46
galleries, 2
games, 38, 61, 70, 89
garden center, 80
garden clubs, 81
Garden District, The, 13
garden items, 4, 13, 22, 46, 80, 82, 100, 122, 125, 131
Garfield and Marks, 36-37
Georgetown, 19-23, 58, 86
Georgia Avenue, 58-61
Geppetto Café, 57
gifts, 36, 43, 44, 45, 46, 47, 70, 81, 88, 89, 92, 93, 98, 100, 104, 111, 117, 125, 126, 131
Gilda's Club, 54
glass, 55, 57, 68
glassware, 4, 12, 22, 42, 104, 126
Glenda Gies, 9
Glover, Rod, 11
GLUT Food Coop, 71
go mama go, 10

Golden Blount, 122
goldfish, 64
Gordensbury, 36
Gormies, 64
Gossypia, 91
gourmet mushrooms, 96
gowns, 115
Great Hall, 46
Green Papaya, 52
greeting cards, 14
Guild of Vermont Furniture Makers, 56
guitars, 67
Gulliver's Movers, 120

hair ribbons, 89
Hammonds, 43
handbags, *see* bags
hardware stores, 127-128
harmonicas, 67
hats, 15, 16, 47, 69, 74, 96-97, 107
Hawkins, Judith Leary, 116
Hawthorne House, 129
Heatilator, 122
Hello Kitty, 34
Helm, John, 55
Henderson, Ron, 14
herbs, 51, 73
H&H Bagels, 110
Hillborn Potter, 117
Hillwood, 37
Hine Junior High, 4
Hobo, 97
holiday ornaments, 40, 46, 93
Hollin Hall, 58
Hollin Hall Pastry Shop, 105
Hollin Hall Shopping Center, 102-105

Hollin Hall Variety Store, Inc., 102
Home Depot, 128
Home Rule, 11
Homestead Gardens, 80
Hot Wheels, 65
House of Musical Traditions, 67
household accessories, 11-12, 16, 35-36, 42, 43, 44, 46, 57, 81, 94, 98, 99, 102, 104, 109, 111, 112, 117, 119, 125, 131
housewares, *see* household accessories
Huet, Gerard, 76
Hurley, Hyla, 40
Hyatt, Christopher Clarke, 69
Hyattsville, 69-71
Hyattsville Hardware Company, 70

Imagination Station, 112
Independence Avenue, SW, 45
Italian products, 5, 22, 35, 54

Jackson, Nisey, 74
J Brown & Co, 94
Jean Louis Restaurant, 76
Jelly Belly, 43
Jenkins Hill, 2
Jewelry, 4, 5, 16, 28, 38, 44, 45, 47, 51, 57, 68, 87, 88, 97, 113, 123
Jewish Bookstore of Greater Washington, The, 60
John Mendes, 117
Johnson, Bill, 17
Journals, 14, 23
Judaica, 57, 61
Judith Jack, 47

Kanawati, Joe, 107

Kazmarek, Jeff, 22
kazoos, 67
Kellogg Collection, 55
Kemper, 18
Kensington, 44
Kestler, Helen, 53
Ketchem, Ann, 81
Killarney House, 83
Kinder Haus Toys, 110, 112
King Street, 86, 88, 89, 92-95
Kingsbury Chocolates, 93
Kingsbury, Robert, 93
Kissing Gormies, 64
kitchenware, 12, 90
Koi, 64, 82
kosher, 66
Koza, Stephen, 82
Kurt, Sefika, 31

La Cuisine—The Cook's Resource, 90
La Mystere, 54
La Perla, 54
Laderach, 43
Lafond, Ursula, 130
Lamplighter, The, 94
lamps, 5, 8, 39, 42, 94, 94, 119, 125
lampshades, 39, 94
Langley Shopping Center, 33, 116
Laurel Avenue, 68, 69
Laurenson, Margaret, 122
Lautman, Barbara, 42
leather goods, 8
Lee Heights Florist, 113
Lee Heights Shops, 109-113
Lee Highway, 109-114, 118, 119, 121
Lee Street, 89

Leesburg Pike, 118
Leland Street, 50
Lemon Chiffon & Lemon Twist, 111
L'Enfant, Pierre, 2
letterpress, 25, 26
Liberty, Caroline, 55
licorice, 43
Lin, Maya, 46
linens, 22, 35-36, 45
lingerie, 21, 53-54
Link, Greg, 11
Lionel, 65
Lisa Jenks, 47
Little Bitts Shop, The, 62
Livingston Street, NW, 42, 43
Livingstone Road, 76
Lorcom Lane, 109
loungewear, 54
Lovecafé, 18
Lowe's, 128
LPs, 27

Mae's Dress Boutique, 115
magic, 58-59
magnets, 14
mailboxes, 122
Main Street, 106
make up, 8
Manaf, Cyrus, 39
Mancini's Café, 101
Maple Avenue, 123
maps, 61
Maralyce Farrar, 117
Maria Scotto, 35
Marimeko, 20
Marine Barracks, 6
Mark Baker Lovett, 28

Market 5 Gallery, 2, 4
Market Lunch, 2, 4
Market Square, 86, 89
Marly Miller, 56
Martha's Table, 117
Marx, 65
masks, 8
massage, 75
Mazza Gallerie, 39
MCI Center, 46
McLean, 33, 34, 115-117
meats, 3, 50, 66
Meeps, 17
memorabilia, 106
Men's Shop Ltd., The, 107
menorahs, 61
Merrill, 44
metal, 55, 57
metal worker, 17
metalsmithing, 88
mezuzahs, 57
Michael Stars, 30
Midori, 25
Mill Street, 129-131
Millennium Decorative Arts, 16
Miller, Judy, 122
Miller, Rosemary Reed, 28
mirrors, 8, 39, 57, 93, 111, 119, 121, 125
Mitchell, Willie Mae, 96
Mohney, Perry, 65
Money Trees, 31
Monier, Toddre, 17
Montgomery Farm Woman's Cooperative Market, 50
Morse Street, 5
Mt. Rainier, 71

Mt. Vernon Avenue, 96-101
Museum of Women in the Arts, The, 47
museum shops, 45
music, 61, 67, 118
music lessons, 67, 119
musical instrument repair, 118
musical instruments, 67, 75, 118
mustaches, 8
Mycrapac, 37
Myers, Joe, 63
Myers, Kathy, 63

Nana, 15
napkin rings, 94
National Building Museum, The, 46
natural remedies, 73
nautical antiques, 106
Navy Yard, 6
needlepoint, 40-41
New Mexico Avenue, NW, 33, 35, 36
New Morning Farms, 73
New York Avenue, NW, 47
Newlands, Francis, 53
Nielsen's Frozen Custard, 126
Nilia, 98
Nisey's Boutique, 74
N. Market Street, 79
North Carolina Avenue, SE, 2
North Carroll Street, 78
North Hall, 3, 4
Northern Virginia Master Gardners, 87
Norton LaTournelle, 56
nose flute, 67
nostalgia, 61

note cards, *see* paper products
notions, 102
Nubian Heritage, 74
nursery, 80-81

Occoquan, 128-132
Old Dominion Boulevard, 109
Old Dominion Drive, 115
Old Georgetown Road, 55
Old Town, 95, *see also* W.O.W. on King Street
olive oil, 6
olives, 6
organic foods and seeds, 73
ottomans, 97
Oui Bee, 47
Oxford Street, 96
Oxon Hill, 75-77
Ozzy Osbourne, 118

P Street, NW, 26
Pachira, 31
paintings, 4, 68, 88
Pam Wright Interiors, 112
Pamela Barkley, 36
Paper Denim Jeans, 30
paper products, 23, 24-26, 38, 43, 45, 70, 75, 93, 98, 103, 111, 129
party supplies, *see* paper products
pasta, 5
pastries, *see* baked goods
Pastries by Randolph, 109
Payne Junker, 56
peasant blouses, 69
Peggy Karr, 104
Pennsylvania Avenue, 2, 5, 14
pens, 14, 24

Performing Arts Store, The, 7
Periwinkle, Inc., 43
personal accessories, 30, 37, 38, 40, 44, 45, 46, 47, 68, 100, 109, 111, 130
personal care products, 15, 36, 43, 74, 98, 104
pet products, 51, 63-65
Philactos, Judy, 43
photo products, 26
photography, 88
pillows, 98
Pirjo, 20, 58
Pixel Blocks, 33
Plaid, 9
plants, 13, 31, 51, 80-81, 87, 100
Plotsky, 42
Point of It All, The, 40
Pollard, Nancy Purves, 90
Pollo a la Brasa, 114
Polly Sue's Vintage Shop, 68
ponds, 64, 82-83
Post, Marjorie Merriweather, 37
Potomac Mills, 128
Potomac West Interiors & Antique Gallery, 99
pottery, 22, 43, 68, 87, 88, 92, 117, 126
prayer shawls, 61
Price, Shannon Denny, 116
Prince Street, 111
Prince, Sally, 111
prints, 27, 46
produce, 2, 50
Protea, 31
public market, 2
Pulp, 14
Pulp on the Hill, 6, 14

Purcellville, 132

quilting fabric, 102
quilts, 92

R Street, NW, 29
Radio Flyer, 34
records, 27
Red Orchard, 55
Remix, 98
reptiles, 64
restaurants, 4, 9, 13, 18, 29, 52, 57, 69, 79, 83
Rhode Island Avenue, 71
ribbons, 14, 23, 25
Riguad, 36
Ritter, 34
robots, 65
Rockville, 26
Roger de la Borde, 25
Rooms with a View, 23
Royal Street, 91
rubber nurse's dress, 21
Rubenstein, Paul and Marti, 25
rugs, 112, 119
Rundholtz, 20
Russ Behrens, 130
Ruth, 30

Samuel S. Case, 132
Sara Schneidman, 47, 98
sauces, 6
sausage, 6
Savory, 69
Schilke, Bob and Ann, 62
sculpture, 8, 57, 68, 88
seafood, 51

Second Saturday, 6
Second Story Books, 26, 58
Sequel, 55
Serenity Space, 75
sex toys, 21
Shalom Strictly Kosher Market, 66
ship's caps, 106
Ship's Hatch, Inc., 106
shoes, 8, 17, 21, 31, 40, 44, 111
Showcase Aquarium, 63
shower curtain, 12
side chests, 39
Signoria, 36
silk flowers, 81, 94
silver, 42
Simon Pierce, 22
sleepware, 9, 35, 54
slot cars, 65
Smith, Charles E., 105, 106
Smithsonian Institution, 45
soaps, 4, 38, 70, 74, 94, 98, 104
sofas, 97, 119
South Hall, 2, 3
South Moon Under, 55
South Park Avenue, 53
spices, 6
Spring Flower Show, 81
Springfield, 127-128
Star's Beads, Ltd., 123
Starfish Café, 9
stationery, 14, 23, 24-26, 38, 129
St. Elmo Avenue, 30
St. Elmo's Coffee Pub, 101
St. John, 108
Studio Z Mendocino, 56
stuff, 125
Stypeck, Alan, 26

Suited for Change, 117
Sullivan, Ann, 35
Summer Delights, 69
Susan Bradford, 56
Sutton Place Gourmet, 55
S. Washington Street, 118
sweets, *see* candy, chocolates, confections
swimwear, 54
Swordtails, 64
Sylene, 53

table linens, 22, 35
tables, 5, 39, 107, 111, 119, 133
tableware, 4, 11, 37, 111, 125
Takoma Park, 66-69
Tarina Tarantino, 30
Tasting Room, The, 79
Taylor, Barry, Susan and Frankie, 58-59
tchotchkes, 94, 117
Teacup Stingray, 64
Teaism, 29
teas, 45, 51, 73
Teleflora, 104
Ten Thousand Villages, 92
Terrell, Lynn, 72
Tetras, 64
textiles, 16, 45, 47, 78-79, 93
Teymouran, John, 39
theater books and scripts, 7
Three Dog Bakery, 51
Three Pigs Barbecue, 117
Thurmont, 77
Thymes, 36, 104
ties, 107, 111
Toast and Strawberries, 28

Gotta Shop! 144

Tops of Old Town, Inc., 96
Torah cards, 61
Torah scroll, 61
Torpedo Factory Arts Center, The, 88
towels, 35-36
Toy Exchange, The, 65
toys, 33-34, 46, 65-66, 70, 88, 89, 92, 109, 110
trains, 65
trash cans, 12
Tree Top Toys, 33, 117
Triangle Lane, 61-66
Trickling Springs Dairy, 73
trim, 79
Trimber, Dorothy, 104
Tropic Bay Water Gardens, 82
Tuscarora Farms, 73
Two Star Dog, 130
Tyson's Corner, 123

Union Street, 88
United Nude, 18
University Boulevard, 58, 66
Upscale Resale Quality Consignments, 119
Uptown Theatre, 37
Urban Oxide, 74
U Street, NW, 13, 15-18

Van Landingham, Marian, 88
variety stores, 102, 103
Vennell, Charles (Ben) and Ann, 102
Vera Bradley, 37, 104, 111
Vermont, 55
Vermont Castings, 122
videos, 27, 59
Vienna, 123-126

Viers Mill Road, 58
vintage clothing, 15, 17, 38, 68, 98
vintage toys, 65
Virginia Grill, The, 132
Votivo, 36

Wake Up Little Susie, 38
Washington Street, 92
Washington, George, 86
water gardens, 64, 82
W. Central Avenue, 80, 82, 83
wearable art, 5
wedding cakes, 62, 77
wedding dresses, 17, 91
Weekend Market Festival, 2
Weiner, Cyla, 53
West Main Street, 132
Westover Shopping Center, 103
Whalen, Irene, 16
What's to Eat?, 4, 9, 13, 18, 29, 52, 57, 69, 79, 83, 87,101, 105, 114, 117, 126, 132, 134
Wheaton, 58-66
Wheaton Triangle, 58
Whistler's Peacock Room, 45
whistles, 67
Why Not?, 89
Wiger, Raymond, 8
wigs, 8
Wild Women Wear Red, 17
Wildwood Shopping Center, 55-58
Willey, Bob and Lib, 119
William Arthur, 25
Willow, 44, 130
Willow Street, 50
wine, 5, 70, 109, 110
wine glass clips, 12

Wisconsin Avenue, 20-23, 50
Woodburners Two, 121
wooden items, 92, 117, 126
W.O.W. on King Street, 92
wrapping paper, 14
writing accessories, *see* stationery
Written Word, The, 23, 24

XOXO, 18

Yasuko, 44
Youlous, Joshua, 61
Youlous, Menachem and Eva, 61

Zawadi, 16
Zelaya, 30
Zoob Modeling Systems, 33
Zum, 75
ZYZXY, 56

Attic Window Publishing, Inc. is Washington, D.C.'s local interest publisher. We produce quality non-fiction books for residents and visitors about the metro area's history and inside track guides to enjoying the best our region has to offer. We welcome your comments about this book, and author inquiries. Mail only, please, sent to the following address:

Attic Window Publishing, Inc.
4905 Maury Lane
Alexandria, VA 22304